KNIGHTS OF THE SKY
The link between the heraldry and history of
the
Royal Air Force
Part 3
Support Squadrons - Stations

Barry R Holliss
Illustrated by Roland Symons

1st January 1988

Published by Enthusiasts Publications
Sherington
Newport Pagnell
Bucks

ISBN 0907700.14.4
©1988
B.R.Holliss

INTRODUCTION

The third part of "Knights of the Sky" covers the units in the alphabetical range of support squadrons to stations. The term support is used to differentiate those units with the word squadron as a suffix to or the main part of their name from the numbered and combative units with the same nomenclature. They are not all flying units as evidenced by 5131 Bomb Disposal Squadron.

The main section of this volume however deals with RAF Stations. Many of the names within the book are no more. In this country they have been swallowed up by housing and industrial estates, or have reverted to agriculture with only rotting and crumbling remnants of a proud station remaining to show where they existed. Abroad many have been taken over by the government of the country in which they were an essential part of the Royal Air Force's transport routes or post-war peace keeping role or they have been reclaimed by the desert sands or tropical jungle from which they were laboriously made. It is to be hoped that this part of the series will to some extent keep the names and memories of those places alive.

One of the criticisms levelled at the first two parts of this series was that the colours of the badges were not given in all instances. With the valued assistance of the Inspector of Recruiting (RAF) and Air Historical Branch the colours of most of the badges of the inactive units have now been identified. Where they have appeared in the first two volumes the colours will be shown in an amended compendium of components which will be issued when the series is complete. Badges in this and subsequent volumes will have the benefit of this further research.

Surprisingly it is more difficult to find the colours of the active units for, apart from writing to each Commanding Officer, there would appear to be no way of easily seeing a coloured illustration of the badge. The fullest record available is a coloured negative collection filed by a transparency number obtained from elsewhere. The acquisition of details of new badges is even more difficult for they are advised in a restricted circulation document which does not give the colours. The problems caused by history can account for the difficulty in getting the full details of old badges but there does seem to be a noticable lack of public relations expertise regarding the new.

Where colours are not stated in a badge they can often, but it has to be stressed not always, be deduced. Crowns for instance are nearly always Or (gold); a fountain is azure/argent (blue and white); a torch is invariably enflamed like fire in red and yellow as are the flames under a pheonix; waves of the sea are argent/azure/vert (white, blue and green); a mound or mount is vert (green) and swords in the main are argent/Or, that is a steel blade with a gold hilt and pommel. The term proper is used where the component is depicted in its natural colours.

In the badge component section where two colours are shown divided by an oblique line it means that the component comprises two colours, eg: sword argent/Or indicates a silver sword blade with a gold pommel. The same convention is used for globes where one colour is the sea and the other the land portions, and on books where the first colour is that of the binding, the second that of the edges of the leaves and the third either the colour of the pages or the colour of the script where this is a major part.

It has be to remembered that the badge representations within are subject to Crown Copyright and are reproduced with the permission of the Ministry of Defence, London.

B.R.Holliss
January 1988

Addorsed	wings spread, back to back
Affrontee	full fronted
Annulet	voided roundel; a plain ring
Apaumy	hand open showing the palm
Argent	silver
Armed	horns, tusks, talons, claws etc
Astral crown	crown with four winged stars
At gaze	guardant (of a deer)
Attired	antlers
Azure	blue
Bar	as fesse but narrower
Barry	divided into narrow horizontal segments
Barry wavy	as barry but with wavy segments
Base	bottom of display
Bend	diagonal partition or display
Bezant	yellow roundel
Billet	an oblong, its proportion being two squares
Bleu celeste	sky blue
Bordure	border
Caboshed	affrontee with no neck visible
Caduceus (rod of)	staff of Mercury
Caparisoned	loaded
Charged	placed on
Chequy	in a check pattern
Chevron	'V' shaped fess
Chief	top part of display
Close	with closed wings
Conjoined	joined together
Couchant	lying down
Counter	opposite, the reverse of
Couped	with the neck cut off straight
Courant	running at full stretch
Cresset	beacon
Cross, pattee	with ends couped, but split and splayed outwards
Cubit arm	cut off at the elbow
Decrescent	with the horns of a crescent pointing to the sinister
Demi	half
Dexter	to the left looking at the shield
Dexter (arm)	right arm
Displayed	affrontee, head turned, wings and legs spread, tips up
Embowed	bent at the elbow with clenched fist upwards
Enfiled (by)	between
Enfiled (with)	an object going around another
Engrailed	looped with points upward
Eradicated	uprooted with roots showing
Erased	with a jagged edge to the neck (i.e. torn off)
Ermine	a fur, the black tipped tail of an Ermine
Expanded	spread out
Fess point	centre of display
Fess(wise)	horizontal partition or display
Fimbriated	with an edge of a different tincture
Fleur de lys	lilly with three leaves; symbol of France
Forcene	rearing

GLOSSARY

iv

Fountain	a roundel with 6 wavy white/blue horizontal strips
Fructed	with fruit
Garb	wheatsheaf
Gorged	with a collar
Guardant	head towards the observer
Gules	red
Hurt	blue disc
In splendour	shown with symbolised rays
Indented	inverted 'V' shape
Inverted	with wing tips down
Irradiation	with rays coming from
Jamb	leg
Jesse	thong holding hawk's leg bell
Langued	colour of the tongue if other than gules
Lozenge	diamond shape
Lymphad	conventionalized heraldic ship
Mask	face of an animal shown affrontee
Mullet	star shape with 5 points
Nebulee	of the clouds, a style of wavy division
Or	gold
Pale	vertical partition or display
Palisado	with projections as of a spear point
Pall	a 'Y' shaped charge
Passant	walking, with three paws being on the ground
Pellet	black roundel
Pendant	hanging from
Pile	wedge shape
Plate	white roundel
Pomell(ed)	knob at the end of a sword hilt
Pomme	green roundel
Port	doorway
Proper	in natural colouring
Quarterly	divided into four
Rampant	erect in profile with hind paws on the ground
Reguardant	having head turned back to look over shoulder
Rising	with wings opened as if to take flight
Sable	balck
Salient	diagonal
Saltire	diagonal cross
Sans	without
Seax	a scimitar with a notch on the back of the blade
Segreant	rampant (of a griffin)
Sejant	sitting
Semee	spattered with
Sinister	to the right looking at the shield
Speed (at)	running
Springing	jumping
Statant	standing with four paws on the ground
Surmounted	with another charge/device upon it
Torteaux	red roundel
Vert	green
Vested	clothed
Volant	flying horizontally

GLOSSARY

Ward   the part of a key which moves lock tumblers
Wreath of the colours   a woven band

MOTTO

MOTTO viii

MOTTO

MOTTO

MOTTO

Acorn, proper	Cosford
Anchor, Or	Eastchurch
Anchor, Or	Mountbatten
Annulet of rope, Or	Malta Comms. and T T Squadron
Annulet, Or	Shawbury
Annulet, azure	Ascension Island
Annulet, azure	Swanton Morley
Annulet, vert	Wildenrath
Annulet, wavy	UKADGE Support Team
Annulets, azure/argent, 2	Khartoum
Ant, desert, sable	5001 Airfield Construction Squadron
Arrow, Or	Scampton
Arrow, Or	Stradishall
Arrow, Or/azure	Armament Practice Station, Acklington
Arrow, Or/bleu-celeste	Martlesham Heath
Arrow, azure	Eastchurch
Arrowheads, 9, gules	Aerobatic Team
Arrows, 2	Honington
Arrows, 2	Odiham
Arrows, 2, (one sable/one Or)	Acklington
Arrows, 2, gules	Staxton Wold
Arrows, 5, Or	Halton
Arrows, 8	3 Ground Radio Servicing Squadron
Arrows, sheaf of, gules/Or	Leconfield
Arrows, winged, sable/argent, 2	Exeter
Badge of Prince of Wales	Brawdy
Balista, gules	North Coates
Barbican, sable	Sandwich
Bars, wavy, azure, 2	Kai Tak
Beacon	2 Ground Radio Servicing Squadron
Beacon, fired	Stornoway
Bear, Black of Berlin	Gatow
Bend, ermine	Watton
Bezant	2nd TAF Communications Squadron
Bezant	5001 Airfield Construction Squadron
Bezants	Kirton in Lindsey
Bird, Canada Goose, displayed, proper	Middleton St George
Bird, Cormorant, perched	Liverpool UAS
Bird, Cornish Chough	St Mawgen
Bird, Crane, rising, argent	Digby
Bird, Frigate, volant	Ascension Island
Bird, Harrier	Nordhorn
Bird, Harrier, hovering, proper	Wildenrath
Bird, Hobby, proper	7630 Flight
Bird, Jay, close, proper	Bicester
Bird, Lapwing, proper	Thorney Island
Bird, Little Owl, proper	Eindhoven
Bird, Mank Sheerwater	Pembroke Dock
Bird, Osprey, wings elevated	Kinloss
Bird, Owl, affrontee, proper	Calshot
Bird, Seagull, argent	Locking
Bird, Snowy Owl, alighting, aff'ty, ppr	Lossiemouth

COMPONENTS

Bird, Swift, volant, Or	UK Mobile Air Movements Squadron
Birdbolt, Or	Aberporth
Birdbolt, Or	Stradishall
Birdbolt, gules	Eastchurch
Birdbolts, 3	Coltishall
Birds, Swans, volant, 3	Armament Training Station, 6
Bomb	31 Bombing & Gunnery School
Bomb, Or	5131 Bomb Disposal Squadron
Book, erect, azure/Or	Acklington
Book, gules/Or	Cambridge UAS
Book, open	Liverpool UAS
Book, open, azure/Or/argent	East Lowlands UAS
Book, open, azure/Or/argent	Wales UAS
Book, open, azure/Or/argent	Yorkshire UAS
Book, open, brown/Or/argent	London UAS
Book, open, gules/Or/argent	Edinburgh UAS
Book, open, gules/Or/argent	Pucklechurch
Book, open, gules/Or/azure	Oxford UAS
Book, open,azure/Or/argent	Armament Practice Station, Acklington
Bow	North Luffenham
Bow, cross, brown	Bruggen
Bow, long, Or	Scampton
Bow, sable	Wyton
Branch of seaweed	Liverpool UAS
Branches of thorn, sable	Thorney Island
Bridge of one arch, Or	Innsworth
Bridge, Iron, at Telford, proper	2 School of Technical Training
Bridge, argent	Bishopbriggs
Bugle	Hooton Park
Bugle	Uxbridge
Bugle of horn, proper	Topcliffe
Cap of maintenance, gules/ermine	Innsworth
Castle, Newark, representation of, grey	Syerston
Castle, Or	Luqa
Castle, Tattershall, representation of,	Conongsby
Castle, double towered, brown	Old Sarum
Castle, triangular,triple towered	Exeter
Castle, triple towered	Chivenor
Chain	Wythall
Chain, Or	Bawdsey
Chain, Or	Idris
Chain, Or	Norton
Chain, Or	Southern Communications Squadron
Chain, Or	Wittering
Chain, argent	Kenley
Chaplet of roses, gules	Cark
Chess bishop,gules	Bishopbriggs
Chinese Dragon, vert	Kai Tak
Church, Cologne Cathedral, Or	Butzweilerhof
Church, St Eval's, argent	St Eval
Circle of chain	4 Ground Radio Servicing Squadron
Circle of chain, Or	84 Group Communications Squadron
Circlet of chain, Or	Biggin Hill

COMPONENTS

Circlet of roses, argent	Hull UAS
Circlet, argent	Stradishall
Claw of an eagle, brown/Or	Air Despatch Letter Service Squadron
Claymore, argent	Macrihanish
Claymore, azure	Leuchars
Claymores, argent/gules, 2	Lossiemouth
Clock face of House of Commons	Metropolitan Communications Squadron
Clouds, argent	Labuan
Clouds, argent	Waddington
Clover, four leaved	4 Ground Radio Servicing Squadron
Collar, indented counter indented, Or	Bawdsey
Collar, sable	Kirton in Lindsey
Column, Roman, broken	El Adem
Comet	Lyneham
Compass rose	Ground Radio Servicing Centre
Compass rose, Or	4624 Movements Squadron
Compass rose, azure	UK Mobile Air Movements Squadron
Cord, gules/azure/Or	Geilenkirchen
Coronet, ducal, Or	Old Sarum
Cresset, enflamed, argent/sable	Staxton Wold
Cresset, enflamed, sable	Fylingdales
Cross, St Andrew, argent/azure	Leuchars
Cross, argent	Cambridge UAS
Cross, maltese	Te Kali
Cross, maltese, argent/gules	Hal Far
Cross, maltese, argent/gules	Kalafrana
Cross, maltese, argent/gules	Krendi
Cross, maltese, argent/gules	Luqa
Cross, maltese, gules	Malta Comms. and T T Squadron
Cross, patonce, Or	Abingdon
Cross, pattee quadrate	Durham UAS
Cross, quarter pierced, ermine	Lichfield
Crossbow	Buchan
Crossbow, Or	Aberporth
Crossbow, brown	84 Group Communications Squadron
Crown, Or	Swanton Morley
Crown, St Edmund's	20 Squadron, RAF Regiment
Crown, astral	Hendon
Crown, astral	UKADGE Support Team
Crown, mural, Or	Castle Bromwich
Crown, open	Aberdeen, Dundee & St Andrews UAS
Crowns, ancient, 2, Or	Swanton Morley
Crowns, eastern, 3, Or	Seletar
Cushion, azure/Or	Medmenham
Decrescent, argent	Oakhangar
Dhow, Or	Bahrein
Dhow, gules	Khormaksar
Dividers, gules/bleu-celeste	5004 Airfield Construction Squadron
Dog, Pointer - demi	Middle Wallop
Dog, Talbot, passant, sable	Bawdsey
Dragon, passant, gules	Aberporth
Dragon, rampant	Valley
Dragon, rampant, gules	Colerne

COMPONENTS

xiv

Dragon, rampant, gules	Wales UAS
Eagle, Bald, volant	66 Squadron, RAF Regiment
Eagle, crowned, displayed	Newton
Eagle, displayed, dark-grey	Geilenkirchen
Eagle, displayed, gules	Port Ellen
Eagle, displayed, light brown	Salalah
Eagle, displayed, wings inverted, Or	Amman
Eagle, doubled headed, Or	Old Sarum
Eagle, perched, sable	Wattisham
Eagle, volant, Or	Kalafrana
Eagle, wings displayed, Or	Kuala Lumpur
Eagle, wings expanded and inverted, Or	Cranwell
Elephant, proper	2 Mechanical Transport Squadron
Ermine, salient, proper	Hemswell
Escallop	Benson
Escallop, Or	El Hamra
Escallop, argent	Spadeadam
Face of a wild cat, sable	Wartling
Faces of a lion, 3, Or	Shawbury
Feathers, ostrich, azure, 2	Brize Norton
Fir cones, 4, vert	Wildenrath
Firebrand	Boulmer
Flamingo, passant, proper	Akrotiri
Flash of lightning, Or	Bishops court
Flash of lightning, Or	North Luffenham
Flash of lightning, Or	Rheindahlen
Flash of lightning, gules	Norton
Flash, Or	North West Signals Centre
Flashes of lightning, 2	Ground Radio Servicing Centre
Flashes of lightning, 2	UKADGE Support Team
Flashes of lightning, 2, Or	Syerston
Flashes of lightning, 2, gules	West Drayton
Flashes, 2, gules	Long Benton
Fleur de lys	Binbrook
Fleur de lys, gules	Kenley
Fleur de lys. gules	4624 Movements Squadron
Fork, military	66 Squadron, RAF Regiment
Fort, arabian, Or	Sharjah
Fountain	Abingdon
Fountain	Ballykelly
Fountain	Bicester
Fountain	Leuchars
Galleon	Bristol UAS
Gannet, proper	Gosport
Gateway, Norman, proper	Brize Norton
Gauntlet, argent	Martlesham Heath
Gauntlet, brown	5131 Bomb Disposal Squadron
Gauntlet, mailed	Coltishall
Gauntlets, 2, argent	Norton
Gazelle, springing, proper	Idris
Gilliflower, proper	Waterbeach
Globe	Lyneham
Globe, azure/gules	Air Fighting Development Squadron

COMPONENTS

Globe, azure/gules	Idris
Globe, azure/vert	Malta Comms. and T T Squadron
Globe, gules	London UAS
Glove, grey	Martlesham Heath
Grenade, fired, sable/gules	West Raynham
Hand, couped at the wrist, proper	Sylt
Hand, couped, gules	Queens UAS
Hand, gules	Aldergrove
Hands, dexter, 2	Stornoway
Head and shoulders of a Centurion	Lindholme
Head of St Edmund	Honington
Head of a Bull (Hereford), argent	Hereford
Head of a beaver, erased, Or	5004 Airfield Construction Squadron
Head of a bull, caboshed, dark brown	Hornchurch
Head of a bull, lowered and affrontee	Marham
Head of a falcon, proper	Detling
Head of a hart, caboshed, Or	Bovingdon
Head of a hind, affrontee, erased	Buchan
Head of a hind, affrontee, erased, Or	Pucklechurch
Head of a horse	3 Ground Radio Servicing Squadron
Head of a horse, (Suffolk Punch) brown	West Raynham
Head of a ram, caboshed, gules	5003 Airfield Construction Squadron
Head of a rhinocerous, sable	Eastleigh
Head of a roebuck, proper	Spadeadam
Head of a sparrowhawk, proper	Manchester UAS
Head of a stag, proper	Swanton Morley
Head of an eagle (bald headed)	Brampton
Head of an eagle, erased	Turnhouse
Head of an eagle, erased, sable/Or	Kirton in Lindsey
Head of an elephant, affrontee, vert	Khartoum
Helm, knight's, argent/gules	Brize Norton
Helmet, (Petatus), Or	Oakhangar
Helmet, Roman Centurions, Or/gules	Catterick
Helmet, Roman, Or	Ouston
Helmet, Roman, Or/gules	South Cerney
Helmet, winged, steel/Or	Medmenham
Holstentor of Lubeck, azure	Lubeck
Horn, hunting	Cottesmore
Horn, hunting	Nordhorn
Hornet, proper	Butterworth
Horse, Pack, argent loaded sable	Dishforth
Horse, argent	Manston
Horseshoe	Cottesmore
Horseshoe, Or	Colerne
Howdah, azure detailed Or	Air HQ India Communications Squadron
Hurt	Amman
Hurt	Calshot
Hurt	Durham UAS
Hurt	East Fortune
Hurt	Scampton
Increscent, argent	Calshot
Insignia, Combined Operations	Servicing Commando
Irradiation, Or	Gan

COMPONENTS

Irradiation, Or	Steamer Point
Jess and bell	Odiham
Key, Or	Gibralter
Key, Or	Locking
Keys, 2, Or	Ballykelly
Khunjar	Habbaniya
Khunjar, sable/Or	Sharjah
Khunjars, sheaved, sable/Or, 2	Salalah
Knight - demi, in armour	Te Kali
Knight in armour	Duxford
Kris, argent	Butterworth
Kris, gules	Kuala Lumpur
Lantern of Crown Tower, Or	Aberdeen UAS
Lantern, sable detailed Or	Drem
Leaf, maple, Or	Digby
Lighthouse, argent	Sylt
Lighthouse, sable	Bishops Court
Lighthouse, sable/Or	Locking
Lincoln Imp, vert	2503 R. Aux. A.F.Regt
Lion - demi	Aberdeen, Dundee & St Andrews UAS
Lion - demi, Singhalese,	Negombo
Lion - demi, winged, gules	Rheindhalen
Lion, couchant guardant, gules	Nicosia
Lion, double - headed, rampant	Birmingham UAS
Lion, passant guardant, Or	Horsham St Faith
Lion, passant guardant, Or	Tangmere
Lion, passant guardant, brown	Cambridge UAS
Lion, rampant	Benson
Lion, rampant	Upwood
Lion, rampant, Or	Armament Practice Station, Acklington
Lion, rampant, argent/sable	Cark
Lion, rampant, gules	Acklington
Lion, rampant, purpure	Ouston
Lion, rampant, triple queued	Wittering
Lion, sejant rampant,	31 Bombing & Gunnery School
Lion, statant guardant, azure	Andover
Lion, statant guardant, azure	Binbrook
Lion, winged, rampant, Or	Laarbruch
Log, Or	2 Mechanical Transport Squadron
Mascle, Or	St Andrews UAS
Mast and sail	Greenock
Mitre, Or/gules	Episkopi
Mound	Binbrook
Mound	Bovingdon
Mound	Brampton
Mound of cobbles, sable	Lubeck
Mound, vert	Old Sarum
Mount	Southampton UAS
Mount	St Eval
Mount	St Mawgen
Mount	Upwood
Mountain, Kinabula, sable	Labuan
Mullet	Cottesmore

COMPONENTS

Mullet, argent	Bassingbourn
Mullets, 04, argent	Calshot
Mullets, 14, Or	Rheindahlen
Pace Stick	Uxbridge
Pall, couped and reversed, gules	Seletar
Pallets, argent, wavy, 2	Laarbruch
Parangs, argent/gules, 2	Labuan
Pegasus	Duxford
Pellets, 3	Bawdsey
Pentagon, vert/bleu-celeste	Catterick
Pheasant, Argus, proper	Tengah
Pheasant, proper	Feltwell
Pheonix, Or	Krendi
Pillar	Southampton UAS
Pillars, 2, light grey	High Wycombe
Plate	Aerobatic Team
Plate	Kai Tak
Pomme	Laarbruch
Port	Odiham
Portcullis	2 Ground Radio Servicing Squadron
Portcullis	Odiham
Portcullis	Valley
Portcullis	West Malling
Portcullis, Or	Gatow
Portcullis, Or	Hornchurch
Portcullis, azure	Sandwich
Portcullis, chained, Or	Wartling
Portcullis, chained, sable	Kenley
Portcullis, sable	Horsham St Faith
Propeller, three bladed, Or	Berka
Propeller, wooden, proper	Halton
Pterodactyl, rising	Upavon
Quarrell, azure	84 Group Communications Squadron
Quill pen	Handling Squadron
Quill pens, 6, argent/azure	Southern Communications Squadron
Quiver of arrows, brown/gules/azure	Nottingham UAS
Ra	Middle East Communications Squadron
Ram, charging, Or	Gaydon
Rapier	20 Squadron, RAF Regiment
Raven	Maintenance Command Comms. Squadron
Ray of lightning, Or	North Coates
Ribbon, sable	Leconfield
Rifles, brown, 2	2503 Squadron R.Aux. A.F.Regt.
Rock	Kinloss
Rock	Pembroke Dock
Rock, grey	Bishops Court
Rock, grey	Mountbatten
Rock, proper	Cranwell
Rocks	Upavon
Rod of Aesculapius, gules	2nd TAF Communications Squadron
Rod of Caduceus, azure	2nd TAF Communications Squadron
Rose, Tudor	Aldergrove
Rose, argent	Armament Training Station, 1

COMPONENTS

Rose, argent	Church Fenton
Rose, argent	Driffield
Rose, argent	Finningley
Rose, argent	Fylingdales
Rose, argent	Linton on Ouse
Rose, argent	Topcliffe
Rose, argent	Yorkshire UAS
Rose, gules	Kenley
Rose, gules	North West Signals Centre
Rose, gules	Waterbeach
Roundel barry wavy	Chivenor
Roundel barry wavy of 8, arg/azure/Or	Steamer Point
Roundel, Or	Rheindahlen
Roundel, argent/sable	Staxton Wold
Roundel, azure	Shawbury
Roundel, azure	Watton
Roundel, chequy	Te Kali
Roundel, gules/sable	Bruggen
Roundel, sable	Oakhangar
Sail, argent/Or	Port Ellen
Saltire, argent	East Fortune
Saltire, argent/azure	East Lowlands UAS
Saltire, argent/azure	St Andrews UAS
Saltire, argent/azure	Turnhouse
Scimitar, Or	Amman
Scroll of parchment, proper	Air Despatch Letter Service Squadron
Scroll of parchment, proper	North West Signals Centre
Sea dragon, azure/gules	Brawdy
Seax, gules	Fighter Command Communications Sq'dn
Sedan chair	Metropolitan Communications Squadron
Serpent, vert	Manchester UAS
Shaft	Lindholme
Shell, azure	Driffield
Shepherds crooks, 2, Or	West Drayton
Ship - demi	Wattisham, Or
Sparks, electric, 3	2 Ground Radio Servicing Squadron
Spears, tilting, 3	Church Fenton
Sphinx, Greek, gules	Leeds UAS
Sprig of broom, proper	Castle Bromwich
Sprig of oak	Finningley
Sprig of olive, proper	Glasgow UAS
Sprig of thorn	El Adem
Staff of St Christopher, brown	Bahrein
Staff of St Christopher, brown	Far East Communications Squadron
Staff, Bedels, argent	Oxford UAS
Stag, salient, azure/Or	Bassingbourn
Stag, trippant	Southampton UAS
Star of eight points, azure	Hendon
Star of eight points, gules/argent	Field Repair & Service Flight, Seletar
Star of four points, azure/argent	Gutersloh
Starfish, Or	Changi
Stock of a tree, proper	7630 Flight
Sun in splendour, Or	Far East Communications Squadron

COMPONENTS

Sun in splendour, Or	Khormaksar
Sun in splendour, Or	Wyton
Sword	Brawdy
Sword	Hooton Park
Sword	UKADGE Support Team
Sword, Iron age, argent/Or	Watton
Sword, ancient, argent	Middleton St George
Sword, argent/Or	Abingdon
Sword, argent/Or	Biggin Hill
Sword, argent/Or	Chivenor
Sword, argent/Or	East Fortune
Sword, argent/Or	Episkopi
Sword, argent/Or	Glasgow UAS
Sword, argent/Or	Martlesham Heath
Sword, argent/Or	Northolt
Sword, argent/Or	Oxford UAS
Sword, argent/Or	Southern Communications Squadron
Sword, argent/Or	Wales UAS
Sword, argent/Or	West Drayton
Sword, argent/Or	West Raynham
Sword, argent/Or	Wyton
Sword, azure/Or	Innsworth
Sword, azure/Or	Sylt
Sword, gules	Horsham St Faith
Sword, gules/argent	Leeming
Swords, 2, argent/Or	Tangmere
Swords, 3	Linton on Ouse
Theodolite, Roman, Or	5003 Airfield Construction Squadron
Thistle, proper	Edinburgh UAS
Thunderbolt, gules/Or/azure	High Wycombe
Torch	Armament Training Station, 1
Torch	Brampton
Torch	Hull UAS
Torch	Queens UAS
Torch, Or	2 School of Technical Training
Torch, Or	Chivenor
Torch, argent	Syerston
Torch, azure	Hullavington
Torch, azure	Wythall
Torches, 2	Newton
Torches, 2, argent	Detling
Tower	Coltishall
Tower, Lincoln Cathedral, Or	Waddington
Tower, St Leonards West Malling	West Malling
Tower, round, grey	Mountbatten
Tower, triple towered	Aberdeen, Dundee & St Andrews UAS
Tower, triple towered, Or	Long Benton
Towers, 2	Odiham
Towers, 2, azure	Ascension Island
Tree, beech, proper	Bovingdon
Tree, oak	Maintenance Command Comms. Squadron
Tree, oak, eradicated, Or	Andover
Tree, oak, eradicated, proper	Cosford

COMPONENTS

Tree, palm, proper	Gan
Trees, oak, hurst of	Brampton
Trees, oak, hurst of	Upwood
Triangle, equilatoral, gules/argent	El Hamra
Trident	Kinloss
Trumpet, Or	Geilenkirchen
Turtle, azure	Masirah
Water barry wavy	Bassingbourn
Water barry wavy	Bristol UAS
Water barry wavy	Gibralter
Water barry wavy	Lubeck
Water barry wavy of 4	Butzweilerhof
Water barry wavy of 4	Macrihanish
Water, representation of	Akrotiri
Waves of the sea	Bahrein
Waves of the sea	Hal Far
Weather vane, Or	Fighter Command Communications Sq'dn
Wheel, azure	Lichfield
Wheel, azure/Or	Northolt
Wheel, brown	Air Fighting Development Squadron
Wheel, cogged	Ground Radio Servicing Centre
Wheel, ships, light brown	Berka
Wheel, spinning, gules	Gutersloh
Wings conjoined in base	20 Squadron, RAF Regiment
Wings conjoined in base	4624 Movements Squadron
Wings conjoined in base	Handling Squadron
Wings conjoined in base	Manston
Wings conjoined in base	Queens UAS
Wings conjoined in base, Or	Nicosia
Wings conjoined in base, azure	Episkopi
Wreath of laurel	Halton
Wyvern, Or/gules	Hullavington

COMPONENTS

A	Arabic
C	Chinese
Cu	Cuneiform
Cz	Czech
E	Eskimo
F	French
G	German
Ga	Gaelic
H	Greek
L	Latin
LS	Lallan Scottish
M	Malay
Ma	Mashona
Mt	Maltese
NL	Dutch
P	Portugese
Si	Singhalese
Sw	Swahili
W	Welsh

LANGUAGE

ROYAL AIR FORCE SERVICING COMMAND
1942 - 1946

SCHOOL OF TECHNICAL TRAINING ROYAL AIR FORCE
SCIENTIA PONS PERPETUUS EST

FIELD REPAIR AND SALVAGE FLIGHT R.A.F. SELETAR
ALICUBIQUAD TEMPORIS

SOUTHERN SECTOR OPERATIONS CENTRE SINGAPORE ROYAL AIR FORCE
MENCHARI DENGAN SUNYI

SUPPLY CONTROL CENTRE ROYAL AIR FORCE
SPEED WITH ACCURACY

WING HEADQUARTERS ROYAL AIR FORCE REGIMENT
PRAEPAREMUS BELLUM

COUNTY OF LINCOLN SQUADRON ROYAL AUXILIARY AIR FORCE
LIBERTAS COELORUM ET AGRORUM

GROUND RADIO SERVICING CENTRE ROYAL AIR FORCE
STRIVE TO MAINTAIN

NORTH WEST SIGNALS CENTRE ROYAL AIR FORCE
CELER ET FIDELIS

ADDENDUM TO PREVIOUS VOLUMES

SERVICING COMMANDO History The Servicing Commando unit was a joint services operation involved in front line work and which existed during 1942 - 1946. **Badge** (1987) Within a wreath of laurel leaves a standard RAF badge frame, the top half in bleu-celeste the bottom half gules containing the Combined Operations insignia of an anchor, rifle and eagle all gules upon a hurt. **Motto** None, the dates of operation (1942 - 1946) appear instead. **Link** The laurel leaves indicate an extinct unit whilst the insignia is that given to Servicing Commandos at the end of their training at the Combined Operations Centre, Inverary. **Motto** None, the dates through which the unit operated (1942 - 1946) appear instead.

NO. 2 SCHOOL OF TECHNICAL TRAINING At Cosford when the badge was authorised **Badge** (3/87) Upon a torch erect Or enflamed gules a representation of the Iron Bridge at Telford proper. **Motto** (L) Knowledge is a lasting bridge **Link** The *torch* signifies the teaching of the unit whilst the *bridge* reflects upon the location near to the birthplace of the industrial revolution and it is therefore symbolic of training as a bridge between the airman recruit and the skilled technician.

FIELD REPAIR AND SALVAGE FLIGHT RAF STATION SELETAR. An unofficial badge of an eight pointed star shaded gules/argent upon a field vert with the motto "Alicubiquad Temporus" was worn by ten individual members of this unit, who had gold wire and coloured silk versions made for wearing on their blazers. It is understood that this badge was in use, at least, in 1956 and 1957

SOUTHERN SECTOR OPERATIONS CENTRE - SINGAPORE An amended badge is shown with the correct bat's mask.

SUPPLY CONTROL CENTRE An amended badge is shown with the magnetic fields shown as a network on the lines of latitude and longtitude rather than as two circles around the globe.

NO. 3 WING HEADQUARTERS ROYAL AIR FORCE REGIMENT An amended drawing showing the correct positioning of the wings is included.

NO 2503 (COUNTY OF LINCOLN) SQUADRON ROYAL AUXILIARY AIR FORCE REGIMENT Badge (9/87) In front of two rifles proper in saltire a Lincoln Imp, vert. **Motto** (L) Liberty in the sky and on the earth **Link** The squadron includes the *rifles* as they form part of the badge of the RAF Regiment whilst the *Lincoln Imp* is indicative of the county and the location.

NO 2622 (HIGHLAND) SQUADRON ROYAL AUXILIARY AIR FORCE REGIMENT The unit was formed on 1/7/79 and the badge awarded in 1985 rather than as indicated in Volume 2.

GROUND RADIO SERVICING CENTRE Badge (12/85) In front of a cogged wheel two flashes of lightning salterwise surmounted of a compass rose of the cardinal points. **Link** The *wheel and flashes* allude to the electrical and mechanical trades involved in the work of the unit whilst the *compass rose* indicates the world wide area of operations. The colours of azure, gules and bleu-celeste represent the joint services nature of the unit

NORTH WEST SIGNALS CENTRE History Formed 15/11/51 at Blackbrook the unit changed its name in December 1970 to Northern Communications Centre and in 7/66 to North West Communications Centre. **Badge** (8/55) In front of a scroll of parchment proper a flash Or in

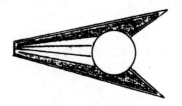

1417 Flight

Badge illustration
to be in Volume 4

bend overall a rose gules seeded vert. **Motto** (L) Speedy and loyal. **Link** The *rose* indicates the location of the unit in Lancashire whilst the *scroll* represents the messages carried and the *flash* the electronic means of doing this.

1417 FLIGHT Although no badge was awarded to this unit Hawker Hunter FR10 aircraft (XF460) was observed carrying at (1) a 3'0" long flattened end arrowhead outlined in white with bars of black, blue, yellow, green and black from the top downwards. At the root of the arrowhead a white circle contained the Khormaksar station badge of a red dhow in front of a yellow sun.

7630 FLIGHT RAFVR Badge (2/86) Upon the stock of a tree a Hobby (Falco Subbuteo) contourne all proper. **Link** The units role is that of specialized interrogation and the use of this bird of prey which has a predatory nature is considered a suitable device. The *Hobby* is also used as the unit's personnel do mainly part-time duties.

NO. 31 BOMBING AND GUNNERY SCHOOL (Pembrey 5/40) **Badge** (4/43) A lion sejant rampant holding in the forepaws a bomb. **Motto** (L) I prepare war among the clouds. **Link** The *lion* alludes to the United Kingdom whilst the *bomb* the role of the unit.

NO 20 SQUADRON ROYAL AIR FORCE REGIMENT Badge (12/86) A pair of wings conjoined in base surmounted by a rapier erect enfiled with a representation of the crown of St Edmund. **Link** The *rapier* alludes to the Rapier missiles deployed by the unit in the defence of USAF bases in the United Kingdom. The *crown* is representative of the location of the unit near Bury St Edmunds whilst the *wings* are symbolic of the R.A.F.

NO. 66 SQUADRON ROYAL AIR FORCE REGIMENT Badge (12/66) A bald eagle volant with the dexter leg extended grasping a military fork bendwise. **Link** The unit is employed to guard USAF bases within the United Kingdom and the *bald-headed eagle* alludes to this whilst the *military fork* generally indicates the offensive and defensive role of the unit.

Air Fighting Development Squadron

NEVER DETERRED

PROGRESS BY ENDEAVOUR

FIT VIA VI

OPERA VICTRIX

OMNIA AD AEDIFICATIONEM

E NOCENTIBUS INNOCENTIA

MAGNOS VEHERE

THE SUN NEVER SETS

EVERYWHERE

IN NOBIS VINCULUM

AIR DESPATCH LETTER SERVICE SQUADRON (Northolt 11/12/44) **Badge** (11/ 46) An eagle's claw erased grasping a scroll of parchment all proper. **Link** The *eagle's claw* represents the RAF whilst the *scroll* shows the role of the unit.

AIR FIGHTING DEVELOPMENT SQUADRON (Northolt 20/10/34) **Badge** (1962) In front of a brown wheel a terrestrial globe, the sea azure the land gules.**Link** The *wheel and the globe* allude to the exploratory role of the unit and its possible world-wide activities.**Marking** On Meteor T7 (WA733), in 1961, a marking of a 7'6" long rectangle of maroon over black was carried at (1). On Lightning F1 (XM137) the same marking, but this time 8'0" long, was carried at (1).

NO. 5001 (LIGHT) AIRFIELD CONSTRUCTION SQUADRON. History Formed 1941 as No. 1 Works Squadron but re-numbered 1/4/43. When the badge was awarded the unit was at Kasfareet. **Badge** In front of a bezant a desert ant in bend sable. **Motto** (L) A way is made by force. **Link** The *bezant* represents the desert where the unit operated whilst the *ant* alludes to industry.

NO. 5003 AIRFIELD CONSTRUCTION SQUADRON. History Formed at Northwood (7/41) as No. 3 Works Squadron with name changes through 5003 Works Squadron to its present title in 1943.**Badge** (10/58) In front of a representation of a Roman theodolite Or a ram's head caboshed gules. **Motto** (L) Hard work is the conqueror. **Link** A Sheeps Foot Roller is a tool used in ground levelling and the *rams face* alludes to this role whilst the *theodolite* also indicates the surveying function.

N0. 5004 AIRFIELD CONSTRUCTION SQUADRON History Formed 12.3.41 at West Drayton as No. 4 Works Squadron but renamed as now from 7/43.**Badge** (12/58) In front of a pair of dividers per pale gules/bleu-celeste a beavers head erased Or .**Motto** (L) Let all things be done unto edifying.**Link** The *beaver* alludes to hard work whilst the *dividers* indicate accuracy.

NO. 5131 BOMB DISPOSAL SQUADRON (Macmerry 21/4/43) **Badge** (3/53) A brown gauntlet holding a bomb Or. **Motto** (L) Out of harmful things, harmless things.**Link** The badge represents the careful handling of bombs which is required when members of the unit are defusing them.

AIR HEADQUARTERS INDIA COMMUNICATIONS SQUADRON (Delhi 1/43) **Badge** (5/47) A howdah azure detailed Or **Motto** (L) To carry the great **Link** The *howdah* indicates the location and carrying duties of the unit for it is the way in which important passengers are carried on the backs of Indian elephants.

FAR EAST COMMUNICATIONS SQUADRON (Delhi 4/44) **Badge** (12/48) In front of a sun in splendour Or a brown staff of St Christopher. **Link** As the function of the unit is to convey passengers east and west of Delhi the *sun* might never set on its activities. The *staff* indicates the safe passage of the users of the unit.

FIGHTER COMMAND COMMUNICATIONS SQUADRON (Northolt 5/44) **Badge** A weather vane Or surmounted by a seax gules. **Link** The *vane* shows operations in all quarters whilst the *seax* alludes to Middlesex where the unit is located. **Note** The badge register description, included twice, omits reference to the seax.

NO. 84 GROUP COMMUNICATIONS SQUADRON (Cowley 1/3/44)**Badge** (11/46) A brown crossbow bent and charged with a quarrell azure, in front of a circle of chain Or. **Motto**

MAINTENANCE COMMAND COMMUNICATION SQUADRON · ROYAL AIR FORCE ·

SAFE AND SURE

MALTA COMMUNICATIONS AND TARGET TOWING SQUADRON · ROYAL AIR FORCE ·

MARE TRANSEO INTERNUM

METROPOLITAN COMMUNICATIONS SQUADRON · ROYAL AIR FORCE ·

READINESS

MIDDLE EAST COMMUNICATIONS SQUADRON · ROYAL AIR FORCE ·

WE TRAVEL THE HORIZONS

SOUTHERN COMMUNICATION SQUADRON · ROYAL AIR FORCE ·

LINK PEN AND SWORD

TACTICAL AIR FORCE COMMUNICATIONS SQUADRON · ROYAL AIR FORCE ·

QUOVIS NOCTE INTERDIU

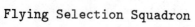

Flying Selection Squadron

GROUND RADIO SERVICING SQUADRON 2 ROYAL AIR FORCE

WE GUIDE AND SERVE

GROUND RADIO SERVICING SQUADRON 3 ROYAL AIR FORCE

ANTE ET ANIMO

8

(L) We form a chain. **Link** The *crossbow* alludes to the speed of the unit whilst the *chain* indicates the joining of destinations.

MAINTENANCE COMMAND COMMUNICATIONS SQUADRON (Andover 1/5/44) **Badge** (8/54) In front of an oak tree fructed and eradicated a raven wings elevated and addorsed.**Link** The *raven* shows the link between the squadron and Maintenance Command (it being the component of that Command's badge) which is alighting in front of the *oak-tree* which forms part of the Arms of Abingdon.

MALTA COMMUNICATIONS AND TARGET TOWING SQUADRON History Formed 3/43 at Hal Far as AHQ Malta Air Sea Rescue Communications Flight but renamed 1/7/54 **Badge** (10/57) In front of an annulet of rope Or a maltese cross gules surmounted of a terrestrial globe vert/azure. Motto (L) I travel the inland sea. **Link** The *cross* indicates the location, the *rope* the target towing function of the unit and the *globe* the communications role.

METROPOLITAN COMMUNICATIONS SQUADRON History Formed as No. 570 Squadron in 1942 at Hendon. Renamed 8/4/44. **Badge** (1/57) In front of a representation of the clock face at the Houses of Parliament a sedan chair. **Link** The *clockface* represents London and readiness to travel at all times. The *sedan chair* alludes to the easy carriage of passengers.

MIDDLE EAST COMMUNICATIONS SQUADRON (Heliopolis 2/44)**Badge** (6/45) A representation of RA. **Link** The *god RA* was also the "Lord of the Air" and "King of Two Horizons". As Heliopolis was also the site of his sanctuary it is considered that he is a suitable insignia for the unit

SOUTHERN COMMUNICATIONS SQUADRON History Formed 1/8/63 upon the amalgamation of Bomber, Fighter and Coastal Commands individual Communications Squadrons.**Badge** (7/65) Six quill-pens quilled argent feathered azure points downwards enfiled by a chain Or: in front of the feathers a sword argent pommelled Or point to the dexter. **Link** The six *pens* represent the six commands who use the unit, the *sword* alludes to the operational units served whilst the *chain* indicates a close link between all parties.

2ND TACTICAL AIR FORCE COMMUNICATIONS SQUADRON History Formed 1943 as 2nd Tactical Air Force Communications Flight and renamed on 1/3/44.**Badge** (5/57) In front of a bezant a caduceus azure and the rod of Aesculapius gules in saltire. Motto (L) Anywhere by day or night **Link** The *bezant* represents travel between the United Kingdom and other NATO countries. The *caduceus* indicates the speed of response of the unit whilst the *rod* alludes to the medical evacuation and transport role.

FLYING SELECTION SQUADRON Although this unit does not have a badge it does carry a unit marking of its own. **Marking** A light-blue disc of 1'3" diameter has been carried on Chipmunk T10 (WD331) on the port side forward of and above the wing root. On the disc is a stylised FSS in red, white and blue, with the name of the unit in white.

NO.2 GROUND RADIO SERVICING SQUADRON (Pucklechurch 15/5/51) **Badge** (1953) In front of a portcullis a beacon overall three electric sparks two in saltire one in fess. **Link** The *beacon and flashes* allude to the electronics role of the unit whilst the *portcullis* signifies its link with Fighter Command

NO. 3 GROUND RADIO SERVICING SQUADRON (Chigwell 22/1/51) Badge (4/56)

GROUND RADIO SERVICING SQUADRON
4
ROYAL AIR FORCE
EMENDATUS AD UNGUEM

HANDLING SQUADRON
ROYAL AIR FORCE
NOTA BENE

MEDIUM TRANSPORT SQUADRON
2
ROYAL AIR FORCE
QUOCUMQUE QUIDVEHERE VELETIS

COUNTY OF OXFORD SQUADRON
4624
AUXILIARY AIR FORCE
READY TO MOVE

In front of eight arrows in saltire a horses head couped. Motto (L) With skill and with spirit. **Link** The *horses head* is symbolic of service whilst the *arrows* coming from the Arms of Sheffield represent the location of the unit in 1956.

NO. 4 GROUND RADIO SERVICING SQUADRON (Chigwell 1951) **Badge** (6/58) A four leaved clover slipped enfiled with a chain circle. **Motto** (L) Flawless to the last degree. **Link** The *four leaved clover*, associated with good fortune, is a link with the number of the unit. The *chain* alludes to the radar chain to which the unit provides assistance.

ROYAL AIR FORCE HANDLING SQUADRON (Boscombe Down 12/4/54) **Badge** (12/55) In front of wings conjoined in base a quill pen in pale. **Motto** (L) Take careful note. **Link** The *quill-pen* represents the reports prepared on new types of aircraft whilst the *wings* indicate the flying role of its officers

NO. 2 MECHANICAL TRANSPORT SQUADRON **History** Formed 17/8/40 as No. 2 M.T.Company and renamed 1/3/54. **Badge** (5/57) An elephant proper passant carrying with the trunk a log Or. **Motto** (L) Wherever you may wish to carry something **Link** The *elephant* symbolises the heavy transport role of the unit whilst the gold *log* alludes to the importance of the loads carried.

NO. 4624 (COUNTY OF OXFORD) MOVEMENTS SQUADRON ROYAL AUXILIARY AIR FORCE (Brize Norton 2/8/82) **Badge** (5/1985) A pair of wings azure conjoined in base surmounting a compass rose of four cardinal points Or the tip of that in chief charged with a fleur de lys gules. **Link** The *compass-rose* indicates the possible world-wide deployment of the unit whilst the partially opened *wings* allude to the movement by air of items by a basically part-time unit.

ABERDEEN UNIVERSITY AIR SQUADRON

R.A.F.V.R.

IN LEARNING IS OUR STRENGTH

ABERDEEN, DUNDEE AND ST ANDREWS UNIVERSITIES AIR SQUADRON

R.A.F.V.R.

UNITED IN LEARNING

BIRMINGHAM UNIVERSITY AIR SQUADRON

R.A.F.V.R.

SCIENTIA DABIT ALAS

BRISTOL UNIVERSITY AIR SQUADRON

R.A.F.V.R.

AUDENTIOR ITO

CAMBRIDGE UNIVERSITY AIR SQUADRON

R.A.F.V.R.

DOCTRINAM ACCINGIMUS ALIS

DURHAM UNIVERSITY AIR SQUADRON

R.A.F.V.R.

DAT SCIENTIA ALAS

EAST LOWLANDS UNIVERSITY AIR SQUADRON

R.A.F.V.R.

ABUNE THE LAVEROCK

EAST MIDLANDS UNIVERSITIES AIR SQUADRON

R.A.F.V.R.

STRENGTH IN RESERVE

UNIVERSITY AIR SQUADRONS

University Air Squadrons are RAFVR units attached to universities which provide basic and flying training to undergraduate officer cadets. These persons need not join the R.A.F once they have graduated. The suffix **UNIVERSITY AIR SQUADRON RAFVR** has been omitted from the following titles.

ABERDEEN (Aberdeen 23/1/41) **Badge** (2/50) A representation Or of the lantern on the Crown Tower of Kings College, Aberdeen. **Link** The *lantern* has obvious connections with the location and background of the unit. **Marking** The squadrons aircraft have carried a motif of a logo style representation, in black, of the lantern superimposed upon a rounded corner square divided quarterly Or and azure upon a rectangle divided per fesse quarterly azure and Or.

ABERDEEN, DUNDEE AND ST ANDREWS History Formed 3/10/81 from Aberdeen and Eastern Lowlands UAS. **Badge** (8/82) Out of an open crown of three visible fleur-de-lys alternately with two crosses flory a demi-lion holding between the paws a tower triple towered. **Link** All the emblems come from the Arms of Universities or Cities. The *tower* from Aberdeen, the *lion* from St Andrews and the *crown* from Dundee.

BIRMINGHAM (Birmingham 3/5/41) **Badge** (12/50) A lion rampant, double headed. **Motto** (L) Knowledge will give us wings. **Link** The *lion* forms part of the Arms of the University.

BRISTOL (25/2/41)**Badge** (10/53) On water barry wavy a galleon its sails charged with the flower of Bristowe, those of the main and mizzen being furled. **Motto** (L) Forward more valiently **Link** The *galleon* is part of the Arms of Bristol and therefore alludes to the location of the unit.

CAMBRIDGE (Cambridge 1/10/25) **Badge** (11/63) In front of a book gules and Or, spine upwards the cover charged with a cross argent a brown lion passant guardant tongued and armed gules. **Motto** (L) We equip learning with wings.**Link** The *lion and book* appear in the Arms of Cambridge University and are therefore symbolic of that City, and the location of the unit. **Marking** On an Avro 504N a blue stripe ran from the engine to the sternpost. On an Avro Tutor the stripe was divided by a thin red line whilst on a Chipmunk (WD379) a blue rectangle was carried either side of the fuselage roundel.

DURHAM (1/2/41)**Badge** (7/52) On a hurt a cross pattee quadrate.**Motto** (L) Knowledge gives wings.**Link** The *hurt* alludes to the sky whilst the *cross* comes from the Arms of the University and therefore alludes to the location of the unit. **Note** The Badge Register omits the hurt in the blazon and that the unit is now part of the Northumbrian Universities Air Squadron.

EAST LOWLANDS History Formed 1/69 at Turnhouse upon the amalgamation of Edinburgh UAS and St Andrews and Dundee Universities Air Squadron (formerly St Andrews UAS) **Badge** (5/72) In front of a saltire argent outlined azure an open book azure/Or/argent **Motto** (Ga) Higher than the lark **Link** The *saltire* symbolises Scotland and also as it was in the badge of St Andrews UAS it remembers that association. The *book* symbolises learning and also the links with Edinburgh as this component is part of the Arms of that University.

EAST MIDLANDS UNIVERSITIES Aircraft of this unit have carried a marking of upon a round cornered square vert a plate charged with a quiver of arrows in saltire brown all superimposed

EDINBURGH UNIVERSITY AIR SQUADRON
R.A.F.V.R.
SUMMA PETUNT IUVENES

GLASGOW UNIVERSITY AIR SQUADRON
R.A.F.V.R.
IN UTRUMQUE PARATUS

HULL UNIVERSITY AIR SQUADRON
R.A.F.V.R.
DOCTI SUPERABIMUS AURAS

LEEDS UNIVERSITY AIR SQUADRON
R.A.F.V.R.
SUPERATA TELLUS SIDERA DONAT

UNIVERSITY OF LIVERPOOL AIR SQUADRON
R.A.F.V.R.
STUDIIS DIVISI VOLANDO SOCIATI

UNIVERSITY OF LONDON AIR SQUADRON
R.A.F.V.R.
LEARN BY DEGREES

MANCHESTER UNIVERSITY AIR SQUADRON
R.A.F.V.R.
SCIENTIA IN ALTO

NOTTINGHAM UNIVERSITY AIR SQUADRON
R.A.F.V.R.
STRENGTH IN RESERVE

OXFORD UNIVERSITY AIR SQUADRON
R.A.F.V.R.
ΑΕΡΟΒΑΤΩ ΚΑΙ ΠΕΡΙΦΡΟΝΩ ΤΟΝ ΗΛΙΟΝ

14

upon a rectangle quarterly of six, azure, vert, Or, argent, brown and brown. The unit used from January 1978 the defunct badge of Nottingham University Air Squadron.

EDINBURGH (Edinburgh 1942) **Badge** (9/48) In front of a thistle proper slipped and leaved an open book gules/Or/argent. **Motto** (L) Youth strives for the highest **Link** The *thistle and book* form part of the Arms of Edinburgh University

GLASGOW Badge (6/48) In front of a sword erect argent hilted Or the point upwards a grey dove volant in bend holding in the beak a sprig of olive vert fructed sable. **Motto** (L) Prepared for either event. **Link** The *sword* indicates preparedness for war but the *dove* is also a sign of the desire for peace. **Marking** A stylised badge in yellow is carried under the cockpit of the units aircraft. **Note** The unit was retitled the University of Glasgow and Strathclyde Air Squadron on 1/1/65.

HULL (18/2/41) **Badge** (8/54) A torch enfiled by a circlet of York roses **Motto** (L) With instruction we will master the air **Link** The *torch* is indicative of learning both at the unit and the University whilst the *roses* indicate the location. **Note** The badge register incorrectly shows the word "Aurus" instead of "Auras" in the motto. **Note** The unit was disbanded on 15/3/69 upon amalgamation with Leeds UAS into Yorkshire Universities AS

LEEDS (Leeds 31/1/41) **Badge** (6/49) A greek sphinx gules. **Motto** (L) Earth conquered gives the stars **Link** The *sphinx* is part of the Arms of the University. **Note** The unit was disbanded 15/3/69 upon amalgamation with Hull UAS to form Yorkshire Universities AS

UNIVERSITY OF LIVERPOOL (Liverpool 12/1/41) **Badge** (1953) Perched upon an open book a cormorant in the beak a branch of seaweed. **Motto** (L) In their studies they are divided, by flying they are united **Link** The *cormorant and seaweed* are in the Arms of Liverpool and therefore indicate the location of the unit. The *book* suggests learning. **Marking** On a plate the unit badge is shown gules all superimposed upon a rectangle party per fesse bleu celeste, argent and sable.

UNIVERSITY OF LONDON AIR SQUADRON (Imperial College of Science and Technology, SW7, 9/35) **Badge** (12/50) In front of an open book brown/Or/argent a terrestrial globe gules. **Link** The *book* as part of the Arms of the University is indicative of learning whilst the *globe* suggests that London can be regarded as the centre of the world from where members of the squadron are prepared to operate when they join the RAF at a later date. **Marking** On a geometric style shield fimbriated sable a cross gules thereon an open book argent superimposed with a globe azure/grey.

MANCHESTER (Manchester 3/3/41) **Badge** (10/49) A sparrow-hawks head proper holding in the beak a serpent vert. **Motto** (L) Knowledge in the sky **Link** The *sparrow-hawk* is indicative of aviation and the *serpent*, wisdom.

NOTTINGHAM (Nottingham 4/41) **Badge** (2/47) A quiverful of arrows (quiver brown, strapped gules doubled brown. Arrows brown, flighted azure) **Link** The badge emphasises the link with Nottingham and Robin Hoood but also is symbolic of the strength in reserve being available if required. **Note** Now incorporated into East Midland UAS.

OXFORD (Oxford 11/10/25) **Badge** (2/51) In front of a Bedels staff argent and sword argent hilted Or in saltire an open book gules, Or and azure lettered Or. **Motto** (H) I walk the skies and keep my thoughts on the sun. **Link** The *book* signifying learning comes from the Arms of the

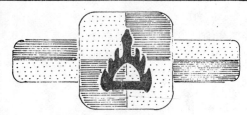

Aberdeen UAS

University of Wales Air Squadron

Liverpool UAS

East Midlands UAS

London UAS

Glasgow UAS

Yorkshire UAS

16

University which association is carried on by the inclusion of the *staff*. The *sword* is indicative of the role for which the personnel of the unit are trained. **Marking**. On a dual-control Bristol Fighter (J8257) a blue stripe was carried from the engine to the tail-plane whilst on an Avro Tutor this was shown from the middle of the cockpits to the stern post.

QUEENS (Belfast 1941) **Badge** (3/49) In front of a pair of wings conjoined in base a hand couped at the wrist gules holding a torch **Motto** (L) To seek new knowledge and new horizons. **Link** The *torch and wings* indicate learning and aviation whilst the *hand*, being part of the Badge of Ulster represents the location of the unit.

SOUTHAMPTON (Southampton 15/2/41) **Badge** (7/51) In front of a pillar on a mount a stag trippant. **Motto** (L) Difficulties yield to gallant men. **Link** The *stag* is part of the Arms of the University and is a link to that institution whilst the *pillar* from the badge of Home Command is the link with the parent Command.

ST ANDREWS Badge (9/51) A saltire argent fimbriated azure interlaced with a mascle Or. **Link** The *saltire* is of St Andrew whilst the *mascle* comes from the Arms attributed to Bishop Wardlaw who founded the University

UNIVERSITY OF WALES AIR SQUADRON (St Athan 26/8/63) **Badge** (7/65) In front of an open book azure/Or/argent a dragon rampant gules grasping with the dexter claw a sword argent hilted Or. **Motto** (W) On the wings of learning. **Link** The *dragon* is the symbol of Wales whilst the *sword* indicates that many members of the unit may join the fighting services. The *book* is indicative of learning. **Marking** On a square quarterly 1 and 4 argent, 2 and 3 vert, a dragon gules surmounting a rectangle barry of five sable, gules, Or, gules, sable.

YORKSHIRE UNIVERSITIES AIR SQUADRON (Church Fenton 15/3/69) **Badge** (10/72) In front of a rose argent barbed and seeded Or slipped brown and leaved vert an open book azure/Or/argent. **Motto** (L) All raised on high **Link** The *rose* alludes to Yorkshire and the *book* to the Universities. **Marking** The unit carries the badge device on a field purpure.

UNITED KINGDOM MOBILE AIR MOVEMENTS SQUADRON (Abingdon 1/5/66) **Badge** (2/73) In front of a compass rose of four points azure a swift volant Or wings in bend sinister. **Link** The *compass* alludes to the world-wide role of the unit whilst the flying *swift* represents the style in which the unit operates.

17

No. 2 Armament Practice Station

18

ROYAL AIR FORCE STATIONS

The following badges are all entitled (unless otherwise indicated) RAF Station suffixed by the location. The prefix **ROYAL AIR FORCE STATION** has, for expediency, been deleted from the script.

ABERPORTH (6/9/44) **Badge** (9/66) In front of a dragon passant gules armed azure a crossbow and bird-bolt in saltire Or. **Link** The *dragon* is symbolic of Wales and therefore the location of the unit. The *crossbow and bird-bolt* represent the missile development and trials function of the unit.

ABINGDON (1/9/32) **Badge** (3/55) A fountain surmounted of a cross patonce Or in front thereof in bend a sword point upwards argent/Or. **Link** The *cross* is part of the Arms of the Borough of Abingdon whilst the *fountain* suggests nearness to the River Thames. The *sword* indicates the fighting spirit of the station.

ACKLINGTON History Formed 1/4/38 as No. 7 Armament Training Station **Badge** (8/57) A lion rampant gules grasping in the dexter paw two arrows one sable, one Or points upwards in saltire and resting the sinister paw on a book erect azure/Or. **Motto** (L) Yesterday it had to be taught, today it had to be carried out. **Link** The *two arrows* indicate a fighting spirit. The *closed book* shows that the training at 7 ATS is now concluded and remembered. The *lion* alludes also to the fighting strength of the station and the nation.

AKROTIRI (1/10/55) **Badge** (8/57) A flamingo passant in a representation of water in base all proper **Motto** (L) The penninsula is always eager. **Link** The unit is near to Akrotiri Lake, a breeding ground for flamingoes.

ALDERGROVE (28/1/36) **Badge** (11/51) A dexter hand gules holding a tudor rose. **Link** The *hand* is the badge of Ulster, the *rose* represents England the whole badge indicating the close ties between English and Irish personnel.

AMMAN (1/4/33) **Badge** (12/50) In front of a hurt an eagle displayed wings inverted Or perched on a scimitar Or. **Link** The unit helped the Hashemite dynasty retain control during an attempted incursion. The *eagle and scimitar*, the symbol of the rulers and the *hurt* representing the sky and, therefore the role played by the RAF, allude to this event

ANDOVER (4/25) **Badge** (8/50) In front of an oak-tree eradicated Or a lion statant guardant azure. **Motto** (L) Power derived from arms and knowledge. **Link** The badge is based upon the Arms of Andover which represents strength, *lion* and performance *everlasting oak*.

ARMAMENT PRACTICE STATION NO.2 Although no badge has been awarded Meteor F8 (VZ494) at [1] was seen wearing a 9'0" long rectangle of yellow with a black stripe outboard and a black spot inboard on the rectangle on each part astride the roundel. On the tail the rudder was of alternate black and yellow bars.

ARMAMENT PRACTICE STATION ACKLINGTON (1/5/46) **Badge** (7/51) A lion rampant Or supporting an open book azure/Or/argent and holding in the dexter jamb an arrow Or/azure. **Motto** (L) Study always to be expert. **Link** The *lion* is indicative of the fighting spirit necessary for an air-gunner whilst the *book* symbolises the learning needed for this role and

ARMAMENT TRAINING STATION
1
1
ROYAL AIR FORCE
ALTIORE PETO

ARMAMENT TRAINING STATION
6
6
ROYAL AIR FORCE
DESTINATA PERCIPERE

ROYAL AIR FORCE STATION · ASCENSION ISLAND
AUXILIUM TRANS MARE

ROYAL AIR FORCE STATION
BAHREIN
IN SOLE LABORATE

ROYAL AIR FORCE STATION
BALLYKELLY
NOS DIFFICULTATES NON TERRENT

ROYAL AIR FORCE STATION
BASSINGBOURN
PRISTINAE VIRTUTIS MEMORES

ROYAL AIR FORCE STATION
BAWDSEY
FIRST IN THE FIELD

ROYAL AIR FORCE STATION
BENSON
SPECTEMUR AGENDO

ROYAL AIR FORCE STATION
BERKA
GUARD SEEK AND STRIKE

the *arrow* the weapons being used.

ARMAMENT TRAINING STATION NO. 1 (Catfoss 5/29) **Badge** (1/39) In front of a torch a rose argent. **Motto** (L) I seek higher things **Link** The *rose* indicates the location of the unit in Yorkshire whilst the *torch* symbolises learning.

ARMAMENT TRAINING STATION NO. 6 (Warmwell 5/37) **Badge** (3/39) Three swans volant in bend **Motto** (L) To accomplish things aimed at **Link** The famous swannery at Abbotsbury is close to the station and the *three swans* not only allude to this but also to the number of components of the unit. One is the HQ, the second is the range party on Chesil Beach and the third the Marine Craft section at Lyme Regis.

ASCENSION ISLAND (1982) **Badge** (10/83) In front of an annulet azure surmounted by two towers of the same one in chief and one in base a frigate bird volant proper. **Motto** (L) Support across the sea. **Link** The *towers* allude to the concept of Fortress UK and Fortress Falklands with the flow and return of personnel and stores being indicated by the *annulet*. The *Frigate-bird*, indigenous to the area has it's wings expanded over the sides of the annulet to show the vital role of the air-force on the island.

BAHREIN (1943) **Badge** (6/58) On waves of the sea a dhow Or, the sail charged with a brown staff of St Christopher. **Motto** (L) Work in the sun. **Link** The *sea and dhow* are closely linked to the life of Bahrein whilst the *staff* indicates safe travel for personnel and aircraft.

BALLYKELLY (1/6/41) **Badge** (8/54) In front of a fountain two keys in saltire Or the wards upwards and outwards. **Motto** Difficulties do not deter us **Link** The *fountain* indicates the close links the unit has with Coastal Command whilst the *keys* suggest the unlocking of knowledge needed to overcome difficulties. The keys also come from the Arms of the Fishmongers Company on whose land the station was constructed.

BASSINGBOURN (1938) **Badge** (10/49) Issuant from water barry wavy a stag salient azure crined and hooved Or charged with a mullet argent upon its shoulder **Motto** (L) Mindful of the valour of our ancestors. **Link** The *stag* symbolises the speed and vigilance of aircraft operating from the station with the *mullet* alluding to the USAF who used the station in the Second World War. The *water* is a pun upon the second half of the word Bassingbourn - a bourn being a stream.

BAWDSEY (22/2/39) **Badge** (1/60) A talbot passant to the sinister sable gorged with a collar Or indented counter indented charged with three pellets, affixed thereto by a link a chain Or. **Link** The *talbot* or watchdog appears in the mosaic floor of Bawdsey Manor and is a link to the location and also symbolic of the role of the unit. The *chain* by returning to the collar reflects the radar role of the unit and the link between the Manor and the Station.

BENSON (2/39) **Badge** (8/55) In front of an escallop a lion rampant. **Motto** (L) Let us be known by our actions **Link** The *lion* appears in the 13th century Arms of the Earl of Cornwall who was the Lord of the Manor of Benson and is therefore a link with the location. The *escallop* is an old device signifying pilgrimage which is relevant to the air transport role of the station.

BERKA (Gianaolis, Egypt, 2/44) **Badge** (10/44) In front of a wooden ship's wheel proper a three bladed propeller Or. **Link** The role of the station in naval co-operation is indicated by the badge.

BICESTER History Formed 1917 as a training depot station. **Badge** (1/58) In front of a plate

ROYAL AIR FORCE STATION BICESTER — SEMEL ET SIMUL

ROYAL AIR FORCE STATION BIGGIN HILL — THE STRONGEST LINK

ROYAL AIR FORCE STATION BINBROOK — UNITED WE STRIKE

ROYAL AIR FORCE STATION BISHOPBRIGGS — BIS DAT QUI CITO DAT

ROYAL AIR FORCE STATION BISHOPS COURT — GUARD AND GUIDE

ROYAL AIR FORCE STATION BOULMER — SEMPER IN EXCUBITU VIGILANS

ROYAL AIR FORCE STATION BOVINGDON — TRUST AND FEAR NOT

ROYAL AIR FORCE STATION BRAMPTON — PRIDE IN SERVICE

ROYAL AIR FORCE STATION BRAWDY — AMDDIFFYNFA Y GORLLEWIN

charged with three bars wavy azure a jay close proper **Motto** (L) Once and simultaneously **Link** The *jay* suggests the storage function whilst the *barry wavy* alludes to the location as this formed part of the Arms of the Bassett family when Lords of the Manor of Bicester in the 12th and 13th centuries. **Note** The badge register incorrectly shows the motto as "Semel et simul"

BIGGIN HILL History Formed 1917 as a radio and later Home Defence Fighter Station becomming an RAF Station on 1/10/32 **Badge** (1954) A Sword erect argent pomelled and hilted Or enfiled by a circlet of chain Or. **Link** The *sword* symbolises the front line fighter station role in 1939-1945 whilst the *chain* remembers that the station was one of many forming such around London at that time.

BINBROOK (27/6/40) **Badge** (7/51) On a mound a lion statant guardant azure charged on the shoulder with a fleur-de-lys Or. **Link** As the unit is located on a hill the *mound* represents this. The *lion* alludes to the national fighting spirit whilst the *fleur-de-lys* is taken from the Arms of Lincoln to indicate its location.

BISHOPBRIGGS History Formed 6/2/39 as No 18 Balloon Centre which was closed on 31/5/43. The site was re-opened on 10/2/47 as No 101 Reserve Centre and renamed as RAF Station on 28/7/52. **Badge** (11/54) A chess bishop gules in front of a "brig" (bridge) argent. **Motto** (L) He gives twice who gives quickly **Link** The badge is a pictorial description of the station's name using the Scottish word "brig" which means bridge.

BISHOPS COURT (17/5/43) **Badge** (1/66) In front of a ray of lightning fesswise Or and on a grey rock issuant from water barry wavy a lighthouse sable. **Link** The *lighthouse* is a representation of that on Rock Angus which is close to the station whilst the *flash* suggests the radar function of the unit.

BOULMER (1/3/43 as a satellite to Eshott) **Badge** (1986) A firebrand. **Motto** Always the vigilant sentry. **Link** Boulmer being a radar station has to be always alert and the *firebrand*, a means of sending a warning is a link with this role.

BOVINGDON (15/6/42) **Badge** In front of a beech-tree proper issuant from a grassy mound a hart's head caboshed Or. **Link** The station is located in Hertfordshire and takes the *hart's head* because of this. The *beech-tree* is representative of those to be found around the station's location in the Chiltern Hills.

BRAMPTON (7/10/39) **Badge** (6/59) On a grassy compartment a hurst of oak-trees fructed surmounted of a bald-headed eagle's head erased in the beak a torch enflamed bendwise. **Link** The *hurst* indicates the location of the unit close to Brampton Park whilst the *eagle's head* alludes to the HQ of Technical Training Command situated there and also the long association that the station has with the U.S. Air Force. The *torch* represents the reconnaissance and intelligence tasks also carried on at the station.

BRAWDY (1971 on transfer from RN control) **Badge** (12/84) A sea-dragon per bend azure and gules supporting with the sinister claw the badge of the Prince of Wales as Heir Apparant to the Throne and grasping in its dexter claw a sword erect. **Motto** (Ga) Stronghold of the West **Link** The *sea-dragon* indicates the location of the unit as it forms part of the Arms of Preseli District Council in which area the station is situated. The blue tail alludes to the previous occupation by the Royal Navy. The *sword* is included to show the parentage by Strike Command and the *Prince of Wales badge* as he is Honorary Air Commodore of the station.

ROYAL AIR FORCE STATION · BRIZE NORTON ·
TRANSIRE CONFIDENTER

ROYAL AIR FORCE STATION · BRUGGEN ·
TO SEEK AND STRIKE

ROYAL AIR FORCE STATION · BUTTERWORTH ·
SARANG SERTA SENGAT

ROYAL AIR FORCE STATION · BUTZWEILERHOF ·
PER VIRES PAX

ROYAL AIR FORCE STATION · CALSHOT ·
DUCANT ASTRA

ROYAL AIR FORCE STATION · CARK ·
EXERCITATIS NIL INVIUM

ROYAL AIR FORCE STATION · CASTLE BROMWICH ·
SUPRA URBEM ALAE NOSTRAE VOLANT

ROYAL AIR FORCE STATION · CATTERICK ·
VIGILANCE AND KNOWLEDGE

ROYAL AIR FORCE STATION · CHANGI ·
KAMMELINDONGI SEMUA

BRIZE NORTON (13/8/37) **Badge** In front of a light-grey Norman gateway a knight's helm argent fimbriated gules crested by two ostrich feathers azure. **Motto** (L) Pass through confidently **Link** The *gateway* indicates the gateway to the world, the station being the main trooping location of the RAF The *helmet* represents the military personnel carried from the station.

BRUGGEN History Originally 135 Wing but re-named 1/1/60 **Badge** (11/63) In front of a roundel party per fess embattled gules and sable a brown cross-bow. **Link** The *cross-bow* is shown in the badge as symbolising the deterrent role of the station, it being located to the frontier of western Europe. The *roundel* is shown in red and black to suggest a fortress which is capable of causing destruction by day or night.

BUTTERWORTH (7/5/41) **Badge** (6/55) In front of a kris argent in bend point upwards a hornet proper. **Motto** (M) The nest with the sting **Link** The *hornet* is believed to be the most aggresive insect common to Malaya and therefore it alludes to the possible spirit of the station. The *kris* is indicative of the location of the station.

BUTZWEILERHOF (1/50) **Badge** (12/55) A representation of Cologne Cathedral Or issuant out of water barry wavy of 4. **Motto** (L) Peace through strength **Link** The badge shows the proximity of the station to Cologne and the Rhine.

CALSHOT (1/13) **Badge** (8/47) On a hurt an owl proper affrontee perched on an increscent argent between four mullets of the same. **Motto** (L) Let your stars be your guide **Link** The *owl* symbolises wisdom and the ability to navigate by the stars. The operations in the air are indicated by the *stars* in the square shape of Pegasus.

CARK (1/42) **Badge** (1/43) A lion rampant per pale argent and sable gorged with a chaplet of roses gules **Motto** (L) To a trained man nothing is impassable **Link** The *lion* is coloured to symbolise the training of pilots by day and night and is collared with a *chaplet of roses* to signify its location in Lancashire. A lion in yellow and green was the main part of the Arms of the monastry at Cartmel near to the location of the station.

CASTLE BROMWICH Badge (6/55) A sprig of broom prper enfiled by a mural crown Or. **Motto** (L) Our wings rise over the city **Link** The *mural crown* appears in the Arms of the City of Birmingham on the outskirts of which the station is located. The *sprig of broom* is a play upon the station name which means 'where the broom grows'.

CATTERICK History Believed to have been formed on 15/9/16 **Badge** (3/71) In front of a pentagon point in base the upper edge embattled and divided fesswise at the lateral points vert and bleu celeste a Roman Centurion's helmet in bend sinister Or plumed gules. **Link** The *pentagon* represents the Castle Hills located within the boundary of the station and together with the *centurion's helmet* is symbolic of a military base once occupied by the Romans but now by the men of the Royal Air Force Regiment. The colouring alludes to the hills and rivers nearby.

CHANGI Badge (8/50) A starfish Or **Motto** (M) We shelter many **Link** The *starfish* alludes to the sea which is on three sides of the station and its five legs to the five major functions located there: HQ, Flying Squadrons, Hospital, Signals Centre and RAF Regiment.

ROYAL AIR FORCE STATION
CHIVENOR
DOCTI PROGREDIMUR

ROYAL AIR FORCE STATION
CHURCH FENTON
WITH SPEED TO THE MARK

ROYAL AIR FORCE STATION
COLERNE
AGE PRO VIRIBUS

ROYAL AIR FORCE STATION
COLTISHALL
AGGRESSIVE IN DEFENCE

ROYAL AIR FORCE STATION
CONINGSBY
LOYALTY BINDS ME

ROYAL AIR FORCE STATION
COSFORD
SEUL LE PREMIER PAS COUTE

ROYAL AIR FORCE STATION
COTTESMORE
WE RISE TO OUR OBSTACLES

ROYAL AIR FORCE STATION
CRANWELL
ALITUM ALTRIX

ROYAL AIR FORCE STATION
DETLING
DARE TO BE WISE

ROYAL AIR FORCE STATION
DIGBY
ICARUS RENATUS

ROYAL AIR FORCE STATION
DISHFORTH
PAR ONERI

26

CHIVENOR (1/10/40) **Badge** (4/82) In front of a roundel barry-wavy a sword argent/Or and torch Or enflamed in saltire surmounted of a castle the three towers conjoined. **Motto** (L) We advance with knowledge **Link** The *castle* comes from the Arms of Barnstaple, the *sword and torch* represent the current and past roles of the station (the sword for defence, the torch for training). The *roundel* alludes to the maritime patrols carried out in World War II and the Search and Rescue duties currently performed by No. 22 Squadron

CHURCH FENTON (16/4/37) **Badge** (4/53) In front of a rose argent three tilting spears points upwards in bend. **Link** The *rose* represents the location of the unit in Yorkshire whilst the *tilting spears* used in medieval tournaments indicate the modern role of air combat.

COLERNE (9/40) **Badge** (11/44) In front of a horseshoe Or a dragon gules rampant. **Motto** (L) Do your utmost **Link** The badge indicates the location of the station near to the junction of three county boundaries. The *dragon* appears in the Arms of both Wiltshire and Somerset whilst the *horseshoe* comes from the Arms of Gloucestershire.

COLTISHALL (1/6/40) **Badge** (1/53) Issuant from a tower a mailed gauntlet holding three birdbolts. **Link** The *tower* indicates the strength in defence of the station whilst the *mailed fist and birdbolts* signifies the aggresive spirit of the fighter aircraft based at the station.

CONINGSBY (7/1/41) **Badge** (12/58) A representation of the Castle of Tattershall. **Link** The badge is indicative of the stations location, the castle being a well known local landmark.

COSFORD (7/38) **Badge** (3/49) In front of an oak tree eradicated an acorn all proper. **Motto** (F) Only the beginning is difficult. **Link** The location of the station near to the Boscobel Oak is indicated by the *oak tree*. The *acorn* suggests the small beginnings from which the members of the RAF will grow after their time at this station.

COTTESMORE (3/38) **Badge** (12/48) In front of a horseshoe a mullet overall a hunting horn in bend **Link** The badge alludes to the location in Rutland with the *horseshoe* and *hunting horn* whilst the *mullet* symbolises the use of the station by the USAF during the war.

CRANWELL (4/18) **Badge** (9/48) An eagle wings expanded and inverted Or perched on a rock proper. **Motto** (L) Nurturer of the winged **Link** The function of the unit is to watch over and protect the personnel being trained there. The badge components illustrate this objective.

DETLING (3/9/39) **Badge** (3/55) Issuant from the upper sides of two torches in saltire argent the head and shoulders of a falcon proper head to the sinister. **Link** The *falcons head* turning to the sinister is in the badge of the Air Training Corps symbolising the training given at the station to young officers. The *torches* represent learning.

DIGBY (13/8/37) **Badge** (7/52) In front of a maple leaf Or a crane rising proper (argent). **Motto** (L) Icarus reborn **Link** The *maple leaf* is included to commemorate the RCAF squadrons which used the airfield from 1943-1946. The *crane* comes from the Arms of Cranwell and alludes to the fact that Digby was used in 1917 as an overflow station for RNAS cadets from Cranwell

DISHFORTH (18/12/36) **Badge** (11/54) A pack-horse argent loaded sable. **Motto** (L) Equal to the task. **Link** The *pack-horse* is the badge of the station for the Great North Road runs past it and many of these animals used to travel the road before motor-transport. A horse is also cut into the chalk of the nearby Sutton Bank and this animal also represents the operational transport

ROYAL AIR FORCE STATION DREM — EXIIT HINC LUMEN

ROYAL AIR FORCE STATION DRIFFIELD — STRONG FOUNDATIONS

ROYAL AIR FORCE STATION DUXFORD — VERRIMUS CÆLUM

ROYAL AIR FORCE STATION EAST FORTUNE — FORTUNE FAVOURS THE BOLD

ROYAL AIR FORCE STATION EASTCHURCH — IN VARIETATE CONSTANS

ROYAL AIR FORCE STATION EASTLEIGH — SHU PAVU NA THABITI

ROYAL AIR FORCE STATION EINDHOVEN — STILTE·BAART·WIJSHEID

ROYAL AIR FORCE STATION EL ADEM — VINCIT QUI PATITUR

ROYAL AIR FORCE STATION EL HAMRA — STRENGTH THROUGH MOBILITY

ROYAL AIR FORCE STATION EPISKOPI — UNITED WE ENDEAVOUR

ROYAL AIR FORCE STATION EXETER — EX AETERNA VIGILANTA VIRES

28

and transport training roles of the station.

DREM (3/39) **Badge** (6/44) A lantern sable detailed Or **Motto** (L) From here went forth the light **Link** The badge in association with the motto is a reference to the fact that a system of night-flying lighting was designed at and named after the station.

DRIFFIELD **History** Opened from 8/18 to 6/19 and then closed to be reopened on 30/7/36 **Badge** (7/51) In front of a York rose a shell azure. **Link** The *rose* indicates the location of the station whilst the *shell* comes from the Arms of the Sykes family who once owned the land upon which the station is built.

DUXFORD (6/24) **Badge** (6/41) A knight in armour mounted on a Pegasus. **Motto** (L) We sweep the skies. **Link** Uncertain, but the general concensus of opinion is that this station claimed to be one of the first to launch large formations in defence of the country in 1940 and at one time was equipped with aircraft powered by Pegasus engines.

EAST FORTUNE (8/16) **Badge** (3/45) In front of a hurt charged with a saltire argent throughout a sword argent/Or in pale the point downwards. **Link** The *Scottish emblem* is indicative of the location of the unit whilst the *sword* alludes to the offensive spirit of the station but is shown point downwards to indicate that it would wish only to defend.

EASTCHURCH (12/11) **Badge** (12/44) In front of an anchor Or an arrow azure and a birdbolt gules in saltire the points upwards. **Motto** Constant through changes. **Link** The *anchor* refers to the long association that the station has had with the Royal Navy whilst the *arrow and birdbolt* represent the air armament used there.

EASTLEIGH **Badge** (3/49) A Rhinocerous' head erased sable. **Motto** (S) Tough and strong **Link** The badge is such as these animals are common to the area.

EINDHOVEN (15/1/51, but previously No. 2 ACRU) **Badge** (9/60) A little owl proper. **Motto** (NL) Silence engenders wisdom. **Link** The *little owl* is common to the area but also is indicative of silence and wisdom which mirrors the secret nature of the role of the unit.

EL ADEM (12/12/42) **Badge** (10/53) In front of a broken Roman column a sprig of thorn. **Motto** (L) He conquers who endures **Link** The *broken column* represents the Italian forces beaten in the area whilst the *sprig of thorn* is included to show the vegetation of the region.

EL HAMRA (4/47) **Badge** (6/48) In front of an equilatoral triangle gules voided argent an escallop inverted Or. **Link** The *equilatoral triangle* comes from the badge of 51 Motor Transport Company which by special permission is included for when it was disbanded its personnel became the MT Squadron of the station. The *escallop* being the badge of travellers is included to represent all those who pass through the station.

EPISKOPI (1955 becoming a station on 15/1/63) **Badge** (8/64) In front of a mitre Or detailed gules two wings azure conjoined in base overall a sword argent pomelled Or point downwards. **Link** The *mitre* is included because the greek word 'Episkopos' means a bishop, the mitre being the symbol of such a person. The *wings* represent the RAF whilst the *sword* alludes to the army, the support of which is a major function of the station.

EXETER (6/40) **Badge** (3/45) Issuant from a triangular castle with three towers two winged

ROYAL AIR FORCE STATION FELTWELL
VIRES ACQUIRIT EUNDO

ROYAL AIR FORCE STATION FINNINGLEY
USQUE AD COELUM FINES

ROYAL AIR FORCE STATION FYLINGDALES
VIGILAMUS

ROYAL AIR FORCE STATION GAN
EN ROUTE

ROYAL AIR FORCE STATION GATOW
PONS HERI PONS HODIE

ROYAL AIR FORCE STATION GAYDON
VIRIBUS VIGEAMUS

ROYAL AIR FORCE STATION GEILENKIRCHEN
CELER RESPONDERE

ROYAL AIR FORCE STATION GIBRALTAR
GUARD THE GATEWAY

ROYAL AIR FORCE STATION GOSPORT
IN CÆLUM VOLANTEM IN MARE TONANTEM

ROYAL AIR FORCE STATION GREENOCK
AL QU A IL - SUAS N'AS THEARR

arrows one sable in bend dexter and one argent in bend sinister **Motto** (L) From **everlasting watchfulness (comes) strength Link** The *castle* comes from the Arms of the City of Exeter whilst the *arrows* allude to the day and night operations of the unit

FELTWELL History In use from 29/11/18 to 1920 as a depot and reopened as a station on 12/3/37 **Badge** (11/63) A pheasant proper **Motto** (L) Ever gathering new strength in our course. **Link** The *pheasant* is a bird frequently seen in the area.

FINNINGLY (8/36) **Badge** (9/48) In front of a sprig of oak a rose argent. **Motto** (L) Extending as far as the sky **Link** The station is situated on the boundaries of the county of Nottinghamshire which uses the *sprig of oak* as a badge, and Yorkshire which has the *white rose*

FYLINGDALES (1/8/62) **Badge** (7/72) Issuant from the centre of an heraldic rose argent seeded Or and slipped vert a cresset sable enflamed gules. **Motto** (L) We watch **Link** The *white rose* indicates the location of the unit in Yorkshire whilst the *cresset*, an old type of signalling device, is included to show the warning role of the station.

GAN (1/2/57) **Badge** (7/65) A brown and green palm tree irradiated Or. **Link** The *palm tree* indicates the location of the unit in the tropics whilst the irradiation alludes to the significance of the unit within the communications network of the RAF.

GATOW (1/8/45) **Badge** (11/63) In front of a portcullis Or a representation of the Black Bear of Berlin (armed brown langued gules). **Motto** (L) A bridge yesterday and a bridge today. **Link** The *portcullis* indicates the protection given to Berlin by the station whilst the *bear* is symbolic of that City.

GAYDON History Formed 8/42 as a satellite to Chipping Camden, becoming an independent station 1/3/54) **Badge** (10/56) A ram Or charging **Motto** (L) Let us flourish through strength. **Link** A skull of an ancient ram was found during excavations for the HQ building and therefore this animal was considered a suitable emblem for when it is aroused it has an aggresive nature.

GEILENKIRCHEN History Formed 1/3/53 but retitled one month later as No 138 Wing. It reverted to an RAF Station on 1/1/60. **Badge** (1/65) In front of a dark-grey eagle displayed an RAF trumpet Or the cord (gules/azure/Or)looped behind the neck. **Motto** (L) Swift to respond **Link** The *eagle* comes from the Arms of the nearby town of Aachen whilst the *trumpet* alludes to the function of the unit which is to be alert and make the first call to bring the RAF in Germany to arms.

GIBRALTER History Formed as North Front on 26/9/39 and re-titled on 27/1/67. **Badge** (4/56) Issuant from water barry wavy in base proper a key Or wards upwards and to the dexter. **Link** The *key* is symbolic of Gibralter being the key to the Mediterranean and is also indicative of the location as it forms part of the flag of the Colony. The *water barry wavy* supports this theme.

GOSPORT (7/14) **Badge** (7/37) A gannet proper **Motto** (L) Flying into the sky, thundering into the sea **Link** The station taught aerobatics and as the *gannet* dives into the sea at a very steep angle to catch its prey this was considered a suitable emblem for a station also involved in the anti-submarine role.

GREENOCK (10/40) **Badge** (4/53) A mast and sail of a ship. **Motto** (Ga) Best maintained only **Link** The badge is indicative of the flying boats serviced by the station. It is also a link with

ROYAL AIR FORCE STATION
GUTERSLOH
VALLIS VESPERIS

ROYAL AIR FORCE STATION
HABBANIYA
INFESTO FERIMUS

ROYAL AIR FORCE STATION
HAL FAR
INTER MARE ET CÆLUM

ROYAL AIR FORCE STATION
HALTON
TEACH LEARN APPLY

ROYAL AIR FORCE STATION
HEMSWELL
BOLD AND TENACIOUS

ROYAL AIR FORCE STATION
HENDON
ENDEAVOUR

ROYAL AIR FORCE STATION
HEREFORD
TAKE THE BULL BY THE HORNS

ROYAL AIR FORCE STATION
HIGH WYCOMBE
NON SIBI

ROYAL AIR FORCE STATION
HONINGTON
PRO ANGLIA VALENS

ROYAL AIR FORCE STATION
HOOTON PARK
DEUS HORAM DAT

ROYAL AIR FORCE STATION
HORNCHURCH
FIRST THINGS FIRST

the location as the Arms of Greenock include a ship in full sail.

GUTERSLOH (1/12/47) **Badge** (1/68) In front of a four-pointed star argent and azure a spinning wheel gules. Motto (L) On the western ramparts **Link** The *spinning wheel* comes from the Arms of Gutersloh whilst the *four pointed star* shows the link with NATO

HABBANIYA (1/37 at Dhibban) **Badge** (1/48) A khunjar Motto (L) We strike the troublesome **Link** The badge links the station with the RAF Iraq Levies which has the *khunjar* within its badge.

HAL FAR (8/29 on Malta) **Badge** (9/43) A maltese cross argent/gules rising from the waves of the sea. Motto (L) Between sea and sky **Link** The *maltese cross* and the *waves of the sea* indicate the location of the unit and the area of operations.

HALTON History Formed 7/2/1919 when the PMRAF Hospital opened. **Badge** (8/81) In front of a wreath of laurel five arrows Or one in pale the others in saltire barbs downward surmounted fesswise of a wooden propeller proper. **Link** The *old wooden propeller* links the station with the RAF of old. The *arrows* come from the Arms of the Rothschild family upon whose land the station was built. The number of arrows indicates the main users of the station; the Princess Mary's RAF Hospital, No 1 School of Technical Training, the Institute of Pathology and Tropical Medicine, The Institute of Community Medicine and the Institute of Dental Health and Training. The *laurel* is indicative of excellence.

HEMSWELL History Built 9/18 and known as Harpswell until 29/12/36 **Badge** (10/58) An ermine proper salient **Link** The station is close to Ermine Street and the *ermine* is indicative of this. It also is a tenacious animal choosing often to fight to the death rather than abandon its attack.

HENDON History On site on 1/4/18 but only becomming a station in 1926 **Badge** (1986) A star of eight points azure the lower ray of which is enfiled by an astral crown Or **Link** The *star* comes from the Nativity star and is symbolic of Hendon being in on the birth of the RAF. The *astral crown* represents the RAF. **Note** The station closed on 1/4/87.

HEREFORD (6/40) **Badge** (8/44) A Hereford bull's head caboshed argent. **Link** The badge is indicative of the location of the unit.

HIGH WYCOMBE (1/4/53) **Badge** (8/66) A thunderbolt gules (charged Or winged azure) supported by two light grey pillars. **Motto** (L) Not for ourselves **Link** The *pillars* allude to the support given by the unit to Bomber Command whose badge is a *thunderbolt*

HONINGTON (3/5/37) **Badge** (6/56) In front of two arrows in saltire points downwards a representation of the Head of St Edmund **Motto** (L) Valiant for England **Link** The *Head of St Edmund* is a link with St Edmunsbury (Bury St Edmunds), near to the station, whilst the *arrows* are symbolic of the Saint's maryrdom and also indicative of the weapons carried by the fighter aircraft from the base.

HOOTON PARK (9/10/39) **Badge** (7/53) In front of a sword per pale point upwards a bugle horn **Motto** (L) God gives the hour **Link** The *sword* comes from the Arms of the City of Chester whilst the *horn* is the 'Wirral Horn' which all symbolise the location and authority of the unit.

HORNCHURCH (8/10/15) **Badge** (2/50) In front of a portcullis Or a dark brown bulls head

ROYAL AIR FORCE STATION · HORSHAM ST FAITH · ADSURGENTES FUGNAMUS

ROYAL AIR FORCE STATION · HULLAVINGTON · SERVICE TO MANY

ROYAL AIR FORCE STATION · IDRIS · SIC VOS NON VOBIS

ROYAL AIR FORCE STATION · INNSWORTH · MULTOS SUSTENTARE

ROYAL AIR FORCE STATION · KAI TAK

ROYAL AIR FORCE STATION · KALAFRANA · NUNQUAM DEFUIMUS

ROYAL AIR FORCE STATION · KENLEY · NISI DOMINUS PRO NOBIS

ROYAL AIR FORCE STATION · KHARTOUM

ROYAL AIR FORCE STATION · KHORMAKSAR · INTO THE REMOTE PLACES

caboshed. **Link** The *bulls head* has a long association as a symbol of the station whilst the *portcullis* indicates the role of the unit as a guardian of London and as a link with Fighter Command

HORSHAM ST FAITH (1/6/40) **Badge** (11/51) In front of a portcullis sable a lion passant guardant Or holding in the dexter paw a sword gules. **Motto** (L) Rising we fight **Link** The *portcullis* is indicative of the unit being part of Fighter Command whilst the *lion and sword* come from the Arms of the City of Norwich on which outskirts the station is located.

HULLAVINGTON (4/6/37) **Badge** (5/72) A wyvern Or armed gules holding erect in the dexter claw a torch azure enflamed gules. **Link** The *wyvern* was a badge used by the Kings of Wessex in which area the station is located. The *torch* symbolises the training role of the station

IDRIS History Formed in 1943 as Castle Benito but renamed in 8/52. **Badge** (6/58) A terrestrial globe azure/gules circled with a chain overall Or a gazelle springing proper. **Link** (L) We labour to serve others **Badge** The *globe and chain* indicate the role of a station as one of the many transport staging posts around the world. The *gazelle* is a local animal quick to respond.

INNSWORTH History Formed 25/4/40 as Innsworth Lane and renamed 27/1/41. **Badge** (11/76) In front of a sword azure decorated Or hilted gules erect in its scabbard supporting on its point a cap of maintenance gules doubled ermine an embattled bridge of one arch Or. **Motto** (L) Home to many. **Link** The *sword and cap of maintenance* come from the Tudor period Arms of the City of Gloucester, which is close to where the station is situated. The *bridge* alludes the parenting role for a variety of units including the Personnel Management Centre.

KAI TAK History Formed 3/28 and renamed RAF Hong Kong in 2/78 **Badge** (8/40) In front of a plate charged with two bars azure wavy in base a Chinese dragon vert armed gules. **Motto** (C) Ability and ambition of the highest. **Link** The whole badge is meant to indicate the location of the unit and that it is built on reclaimed land in Kowloon Bay.

KALAFRANA (7/16) **Badge** (4/38) A maltese cross argent/gules surmounted of an eagle volant Or. **Motto** (L) We have never failed **Link** The *maltese cross* indicates the location of the station whilst the *eagle* alludes to the early use of the station by the Royal Naval Air Service

KENLEY History The site was in use as No 7 Acceptance Park from 6/17 with the Station HQ arriving on 22/9/24 **Badge** (12/58) A portcullis sable chained argent the base partially surmounting a rose gules barbed and seeded the upper part surmounted of a fleur-de-lys Or. **Motto** (L) Except the Lord be on our side. **Link** The *portcullis* is an indication of the succeful defence of London and the stations link with Fighter Command, from which badge the device comes. The *rose and lily* are references to London and Paris to where flights were made, and fights over France in both World Wars.

KHARTOUM (22/4/40) **Badge** (7/53) In front of two annulets azure and argent an elephants head affrontee vert. **Motto** (A) Main road of Africa **Link** The *elephants head* alludes to Khartoum for its name in Arabic means 'trunk of the elephant'. The *annulets* are indicative of the location of the station at the confluence of the Blue and White Nile rivers.

KHORMAKSAR (4/39) **Badge** (2/50) In front of a sun in splendour Or a dhow gules. **Link** The *dhow* is symbolic of local transport and therefore the role of the unit whilst the *sun in splendour* is indicative of the normal temperatures in the region.

ROYAL AIR FORCE STATION KINLOSS
POWER TO THE HUNTER

ROYAL AIR FORCE STATION KIRTON IN LINDSEY
JE VOLE A TOUS VENTS

ROYAL AIR FORCE STATION KRENDI
AD REPUGNANDUM RENATUS

ROYAL AIR FORCE STATION KUALA LUMPUR
WE PROTECT FROM THE SKIES

ROYAL AIR FORCE STATION LAARBRUCH
EINE FESTE BURG

ROYAL AIR FORCE STATION LABUAN
STRIKE AND SUPPORT

ROYAL AIR FORCE STATION LECONFIELD
EX TENEBRIS AD LUCEM

ROYAL AIR FORCE STATION LEEMING
STRAIGHT AND TRUE

ROYAL AIR FORCE STATION LEUCHARS
ATTACK AND PROTECT

ROYAL AIR FORCE STATION LICHFIELD
E SINGULIS COMMUNITAS

ROYAL AIR FORCE STATION LINDHOLME
GUIDED STEEL

36

KINLOSS (6/39) **Badge** (8/54) Standing on a rock an osprey wings elevated supporting with the dexter claw a trident. **Link** The station is concerned with training and connected with Coastal Command. The *osprey and rock* are indicative of the location whilst the *trident* alludes to the Coastal Command connection.

KIRTON IN LINDSEY (11/47) **Badge** An eagles head erased sable beaked Or gorged with a collar of bezants. **Motto** (F) I fly whatever the wind **Link** The *eagle* represents the American Eagle Squadron which flew from the station whilst the *collar and bezants* are a link with the Duchy of Cornwall in which achievement the bezants appear and who owned the land upon which the station was built.

KRENDI (11/42) **Badge** (6/44) In front of a maltese Cross argent/gules a pheonix Or **Motto** Reborn to hit back **Link** The *Maltese Cross* indicates the location of the station whilst the *pheonix* is a reference to the fact that the station was established upon the site of a "shadow" aerodrome.

KUALA LUMPUR History Established on 1/11/45 and in being until until 15/11/47 when it closed. The station was reopened and renamed RAF Task Force Malaya on 1/7/48 and known as this until 20/9/48 when the title reverted to the original. **Badge** (1952) An eagle Or wings displayed perched on a Kris gules. **Link** The *eagle* is indicative of the aerial defence of the capital of Malaya whilst the *kris* represents this city, it being the national weapon.

LAARBRUCH (1/8/54) **Badge** (4/62) A pomme charged with a winged lion rampant Or to the sinister between two pallets argent wavy. **Motto** (G) A firm fortress **Link** The *lion* represents the United Kingdom and the RAF, the *pomme* the wooded area around the station and the *pallets* the Rivers Rhine and Maas between which the station is situated.

LABUAN Badge (2/66) In front of a representation of the Mountain of Kinabula sable issuant from clouds argent two parangs argent hilted gules in saltire. **Link** The *mountain* is a navigational aid and appears on the flag of Sabah. The *parangs* are native weapons and tools

LECONFIELD (12/36) **Badge** (4/44) A sheaf of arrows gules flighted Or bound with a ribbon sable **Motto** (L) From darkness to light **Link** The *arrows* indicate bombs dropped by units from the station and are red and gold to signify their effect. The black *ribbon* indicates night operations from the station.

LEEMING (6/40) **Badge** (4/42) A sword gules hilted argent erect the point uppermost. **Link** The badge represents the fighting instincts of the units at the station.

LEUCHARS (1/8/38) **Badge** (1951) In front of a fountain a St Andrews Cross argent fimbtiated azure overall a claymore point uppermost azure. **Link** The *fountain* alludes to the command of the satation by Coastal Command, the *St Andrews Cross* the location in Scotland and the *claymore* the fighting spirit of the Scottish people, it being a weapon of that area.

LICHFIELD (12/5/41) **Badge** (3/55) In front of a wheel azure a cross quarter-pierced ermine. **Motto** (L) Out of separate individuals a commonwealth **Link** The *cross* comes from the Arms of the City of Lichfield and therefore is representative of the location whilst the *wheel* is indicative of the role of the unit which is mainly the storage and operation of motor transport.

LINDHOLME History Formed 3/6/40 as Hatfield Woodhouse but renamed early on it's life. **Badge** The head and shoulders of a centurion facing and aiming to the sinister with the dexter

ROYAL AIR FORCE STATION · LINTON ON OUSE · A FLVMINE IMPVGNAMIS

ROYAL AIR FORCE STATION · LOCKING · DOCEMUS

ROYAL AIR FORCE STATION · LONG BENTON · VOLENS ET POTENS

ROYAL AIR FORCE STATION · LOSSIEMOUTH · THOIR AN AIRE

ROYAL AIR FORCE STATION · LUBECK · IY SUIS IY RESTE

ROYAL AIR FORCE STATION · LUQA · MITJAR QATT MIRBUII

ROYAL AIR FORCE STATION · LYNEHAM · SUPPORT · SAVE · SUPPLY

ROYAL AIR FORCE STATION · MACHRIHANISH · AIRM A DHIONADH NA FAIRGEACHAN

ROYAL AIR FORCE STATION · MANSTON · ARISE TO PROTECT

hand a steel tipped shaft. (The helmet is Or with a red and brown crest, the cloak gules, the tunic argent and the spear haft brown with an argent tip. **Link** The *centurion* is representative of the Roman legions which were stationed in the area and is also symbolic of the fighting spirit of the military men at the base.

LINTON ON OUSE (13/5/37) **Badge** (8/54) Three swords point upwards the dexter and sinister inclined outwards surmounted by a York rose. **Motto** (L) From the river we strike **Link** The *three swords* represent the three wings and three squadrons at the station. The *rose* is indicative of the location of the unit.

LOCKING History Although No 5 School of Technical Training was formed at Locking on 2/1/39 the station, as such, was not opened until 15/5/50 **Badge** (4/77) In front of a lighthouse sable lanterned Or a seagull argent alighting upon a key fesswise wards downwards and to the sinister Or. **Motto** (L) We teach. **Link** The *gull and lighthouse* come from the Arms of Weston - super - Mare, close to the station and are therefore indicative of the location. The *key* is representative of knowledge.

LONG BENTON (5/6/39) **Badge** (6/56) In front of two flashes gules in saltire a tower triple towered Or. **Motto** (L) Willing and able **Link** The *castle* is indicative of the role of the unit (the safe storage of equipment). It also signifies defence and further is in the Arms of the City of Newcastle upon Tyne, close to the location of the station. The *flashes* allude to the part electricity plays in the function of defence and the equipment kept.

LOSSIEMOUTH (1/4/39) **Badge** (5/74) Alighting upon two claymores argent hilted gules in saltire a snowy owl proper affronty wings expanded and inverted. **Motto** (Ga) To be watchful **Link** The *snowy owl* which is only found in Scotland has eyes able to see in light 100 times less than man. The unit at the station (No 8 (AEW) Squadron) hunts by radar and the owl alludes to this. It is also indicative of the wisdom being given by the Jaguar Operational Conversion Unit. The *claymores* further allude to Scotland and the attack potential of the station they being weapons of the area.

LUBECK (4/46) **Badge** (5/47) On water barry wavy a representation of the Holstentor of Lubeck azure upon a mount of cobbles. **Motto** (F) Here I am and here I stay. **Link** The link is the location of the unit.

LUQA Badge (2/45) In front of a maltese cross argent/gules a castle Or. **Motto** (Mt) An airfield never beaten **Link** The *maltese cross* indicates the location of the unit whilst the *castle* remembers the fortress of Malta which withstood all attacks against it in the Second World War.

LYNEHAM History Formed 25/5/40 as 33MU and renamed 13/2/42 **Badge** (12/55) In front of a terrestrial globe a comet. **Link** The *globe* indicates the role of the unit as an air transport station whilst the *comet* represents one of the types of aircraft employed (DH Comet)

MACRIHANISH History Transferred from Royal Navy command on 27/5/63 **Badge** (5/75) A claymore argent the blade surmounting water barry wavy of 4 **Motto** (Ga) Arms to defend the sea **Link** The badge depicts the role of the station that of a deployment base for defence of the seas.

MANSTON (9/16) **Badge** (12/48) In front of wings conjoined in base a white horse forcene. **Link** The *horse* is the symbol of the County of Kent and therefore alludes to the location of the

ROYAL AIR FORCE STATION
MARHAM
DETER

ROYAL AIR FORCE STATION
MARTLESHAM HEATH
OMNIA ACTA BENE FACTA

ROYAL AIR FORCE STATION
MASIRAH
AL-I'TIMAD'ALA AL-NAFS

ROYAL AIR FORCE STATION
MEDMENHAM
SERVE AND SUPPORT

ROYAL AIR FORCE STATION
MIDDLETON St GEORGE
SHIELD AND DETER

ROYAL AIR FORCE STATION
MIDDLE WALLOP
VIAM DEMONSTRAMUS

ROYAL AIR FORCE STATION
MOUNT BATTEN
IN HONOUR BOUND

ROYAL AIR FORCE STATION
NEGOMBO
SERVE TO UNITE

ROYAL AIR FORCE STATION
NEWTON
DOCEMUS ET DISCIMUS

ROYAL AIR FORCE STATION
NICOSIA
IN QUADRIVIO PARATUS

40

unit whilst the *wings* represent the RAF operating from and watching over the area.

MARHAM (reopened 1/4/37) **Badge** (10/57) A bull the head lowered and affrontee **Link** A *bull* is recognised as aggresive to intruders to its area and as such depicts the role of the unit.

MARTLESHAM HEATH (14/9/39 when A E E marched out) **Badge** (3/60) Two dexter hands that to the dexter gloved in grey velvet fringed and tasselled and grasping an arrrow Or flighted bleu-celeste point upwards, that to the sinister gauntleted argent grasping a sword argent hilted Or point upwards the sword and arrow in saltire. **Motto** (L) All deeds well done **Link** The *sword* alludes to the station having been within Fighter Command, the *arrow* that the station was the home of the A E E. The *gauntlet* represents the units service personnel whilst the *glove* does the same for the civilian staff employed.

MASIRAH (2/4/43) **Badge** (8/62) A loggerhead turtle azure **Motto** (A) The reliance is on one's own self **Link** The *turtle* abounds within the locality.

MEDMENHAM (12/6/41) **Badge** (3/60) A cushion azure tasselled Or resting thereon a steel helmet winged Or. **Link** The *helmet* comes from the Arms of the Danesfield family upon whose estate the station is situated. The *cushion* represents the administrative and domestic functions of a Command HQ.

MIDDLETON ST GEORGE (15/1/41) **Badge** (10/58) A Canada Goose proper displayed holding the blade of an ancient sword argent pommel and hilt to the sinister. **Link** The *goose* alludes to a local area called 'Goosepool' and to the Royal Canadian Air Force who were based at the station in 1939/45. The *sword* being the weapon of St George is a reference to the station's name and symbolic of the defence of the area.

MIDDLE WALLOP (11/6/40) **Badge** (7/53) A demi-pointer **Motto** (L) We show the way. **Link** The role of the station was fighter guidance and the *pointer dog* is symbolic of this.

MOUNTBATTEN History Opened 3/17 as Cattewater and known as this until 10/29. **Badge** (2/42) On a grey rock charged with an anchor Or a grey round tower **Link** The *anchor* is a link with the Royal Naval Air Service which used the base during World War 1. The *tower* is a local landmark.

NEGOMBO History Formed at Katunayake and renamed 14/3/44 **Badge** (11/54) A representation of a demi-Singhalese lion. **Link** The *lion* is the symbol of Singapore and there is indicative of the location.

NEWTON (6/40) **Badge** (7/45) An eagle displayed crowned and holding in the claws two torches. **Motto** (L) We teach and we learn **Link** The unit hosted 16 (Polish) SFTS from which badge the *eagle* is drawn. The *torches* represent learning.

NICOSIA (1/2/44) **Badge** (4/61) In front of wings conjoined in base Or a lion couchant guardant gules. **Motto** (L) Ready at the cross-roads. **Link** The *lion* refers to Venice which has always had a close association with Cyprus. It also is a watchful and alert animal representative of the unit. The *wings* allude to the flying role of the station.

NORDHORN Badge (2/85) A young hen harrier head turned to the sinister and perched upon a hunting horn. **Motto** (G) Scoring wins **Link** The Hawker Harrier uses the range which the station

ROYAL AIR FORCE STATION · NORTH COATES
GUIDE TO ATTACK

ROYAL AIR FORCE STATION · NORTH LUFFENHAM
SWIFT TO REPLY

ROYAL AIR FORCE STATION · NORTHOLT
AUT PORTARE AUT PUGNARE PROMPTI

ROYAL AIR FORCE STATION · NORTON
TEST AND PROVE

ROYAL AIR FORCE STATION · OAKHANGER
ULTRA TELLUREM DICO

ROYAL AIR FORCE STATION · ODIHAM
PROMISE AND FULFIL

ROYAL AIR FORCE STATION · OLD SARUM
SEMPER INTER PRIMOS

ROYAL AIR FORCE STATION · OUSTON
PERSIST

controls for air to ground firing practice and therefore the bird depicted which hunts from the air to the ground is a suitable symbol. It is depicted as a juvenile to emphasise that it has a desire to develop its skills. The *horn* comes from the Arms of Nordhorn.

NORTH COATES History Formed at North Coates Fittes and known by that name until the beginning of the Second World War. **Badge** (10/58) In front of a ray of lightning Or in bend a balista gules. **Link** The *balista* is a bombarding weapon therefore suitable to suggest the role of the station. It is coloured red to represent the Army Co-operation work carried out from the station. The *lightning flash* alludes to radar equipment now in use.

NORTH LUFFENHAM **Badge** (4/62) A brown bow in full draught bendwise and to the sinsister charged with a flash of lightning Or. **Link** The *lightning* is symbolic of Thor, the God of Thunder, and representative of the missiles of that name deployed at the station. The *bow* is drawn to indicate readiness.

NORTHOLT (3/3/15)**Badge** (4/62) A sword argent pommelled Or point upwards the blade surmounted of a wheel azure rimmed and nailed Or. **Motto**(L) Ready to carry or fight **Link** The *sword* is to show the wartime association with Fighter Command whilst the *wheel* represents the air transport station role of the unit.

NORTON History Formed 1/9/39 as No 16 Balloon Centre and renamed 1/6/43 **Badge** (1953) A flash of lightning gules and a chain Or grasped by two gauntlets argent in saltire **Link** As the work of the unit is the receiving and testing of parts of mobile radar convoys it was considered suitable that the *lightning* should reperesent the electronics whilst the *chain* indicates the radar chain of which the units would form part. The *gauntlets* represent the personnel of the station.

OAKHANGAR (20/12/67 upon transfer from the Army. **Badge** (7/74) In front of a roundel sable charged with a decrescent argent a petatus Or. **Motto** (L) I speak the truth. **Link** The unit has a radio communications role and the *roundel* represents the dark continium of space through which the messages travel with the *decresent* alluding to the use of earth satellites for this purpose. The *petatus* (the winged helmet of Mercury) is symbolic of the carriage of messages past the earths boundary. **Note** Prior to 6/71 the unit used the badge of No. 90 Group.

ODIHAM (11/1/37) **Badge** (11/51) In front of a port between two towers each charged with a rose the portcullis lowered two arrows points upwards in saltire entwined by a jess and surmounted by a bell. **link** The *port and towers* allude to Odiham Castle whilst the *portcullis* comes from the badge of Fighter Command. The *roses* come from the Arms of the County of Hampshire whilst the *arrows* represent the speed of the aircraft flown from the station. The *jess and bells* represent a falconer and his bird alluding to the control of hunting aircraft and therefore the type of squadron based at the station.

OLD SARUM History Formed 1919 becoming a station on 1/4/63 **Badge** (12/63) A double headed eagle Orarmed azure displayed gorged with a ducal coronet Or in front of a representation of the castle mound of Old Sarum vert ensigned with a light brown castle of two towers. **Motto** (L) Ever amongst the first. **Link** The *mound and castle* are suggestive of that which was near to the location of the station whilst this indication of locality is strenthened by the inclusion of the *eagle* from the Arms of the nearby City of Salisbury

OUSTON (1/2/41) **Badge** (1953) A lion rampant purpure in front of a Roman helmet Or. **Link** The *helmet* is suggestive of Hadrians Wall which is parallel to the station boundary and the RAF

ROYAL AIR FORCE STATION · PEMBROKE DOCK ·
GWYLIOR GORLLEWIN OR AWYR

ROYAL AIR FORCE STATION · PORT ELLEN ·
AIR MUIR IS AIR TIR

ROYAL AIR FORCE STATION · PUCKLECHURCH ·
ALERT

ROYAL AIR FORCE STATION · RHEINDAHLEN ·
ZEALOUS IN SUPPORT

ROYAL AIR FORCE STATION · ST ATHAN ·
Y SIAFFT I FLAEN Y BICELL

ROYAL AIR FORCE STATION · St EVAL ·
FAITH IN OUR TASK

ROYAL AIR FORCE STATION · ST. MAWGAN ·
VIGILA

ROYAL AIR FORCE STATION · SALALAH ·
NUSOOR FEE ARD SADEEQA

ROYAL AIR FORCE STATION · SANDWICH ·
WE TAKE OUR TOLL

ROYAL AIR FORCE STATION · SCAMPTON ·
ARMATUS NON LACESSITUR

Regiment based there who act as infantry. The *lion* in its colour comes from the Arms of the Percy family strong in the locality.

PEMBROKE DOCK (5/34) **Badge** (1/48) On a rock a Manx Sheerwater **Motto** (W) To watch the west from the air. **Link** The bird is symbolic of aircraft operating from water over the sea.

PORT ELLEN (8/40) **Badge** (7/43) A Sail argent/Or charged with an eagle displayed gules **Motto** (Ga) From land and sea **Link** The *sail* represents the role of the station as a seaplane base whilst the *eagle* does the same for aircraft operating from the base.

PUCKLECHURCH (1939) **Badge** (6/58) In front of an open book gules/Or/argent a hinds head and neck affrontee and erased Or. **Link** The *hinds head* indicates that the station is near to a deer park and because these animals are watchful they represent the training, reinforced by the inclusion of a *book*, given at the base.

RHEINDAHLEN Note Originally RAF Monchengladbach until 1/4/60 **Badge** (7/75) In front of a roundel Or semee of 14 mullets vert a winged demi-lion gules holding in the paws a branch of olive vert. **Link** The *roundel and mullets* come from the Arms of Monchen whilst the *lion* is based upon the badge of RAF Germany.

ST ATHAN (1/9/38) **Badge** (3/71) In front of a cogwheel azure a demi-dragon gules erased grasping a flash of lightning erect Or **Motto** (W) Shaft for the spearhead. **Link** The *cogwheel* is symbolic of the largest engineering facility in the RAF whilst the *dragon* comes from the Arms of Glamorgan County Council in which area the unit is situated. This latter component is also used to represent South Wales and 19 MU whilst the *flash of lightning* is indicative of 32 MU

ST EVAL Badge (10/49) On a mount a representation argent of the church of St Eval. **Link** The *church* is a local landmark for pilots.

ST MAWGAN History Formed 1941 at Trebelzue by which name the station was known until 2/43. **Badge** (10/58) On a mount a Cornish Chough. **Motto** (L) Keep watch. **Link** The *Cornish Chough* on a *mount* represents the geographical and topographical location of the station.

SALALAH (11/11/43) **Badge** (8/66) In front of a light brown eagle displayed two sheaved khunjars sable hilted argent and tipped Or in saltire. **Motto** (A) Eagles in a friendly land **Link** The *eagle* represents the RAF whilst the *khunjars* indicate the location, they coming from the Arms of the Sultan of Muscat and Oman.

SANDWICH History From 1942 a GCI station but renamed 1/11/46 **Badge** A barbican sable each tower charged with three chequy bands sable/argent superimposed upon a portcullis azure. **Link** The *barbican* alludes to that on Sandwich Toll Bridge and is indicative therefore of the unit's location whilst the *portcullis* is symbolic of the protection given by the station.

SCAMPTON History Opened 1/16 for the Great War and inactive from 1919 until re-opened 27/8/36 **Badge** (12/58) A hurt surmounted of an arrow bend sinisterwise and a long bow palewise all Or. **Motto** (L) an armed man is not attacked. **Link** The *hurt* is symbolic of the RAF whilst the other components are a topographical representation of the station. The *arrow* is the lengthened main runway, the *string* of the bow the course of the old Watling Street which passes by the station and the *bow* the realignment of the road neccesitated by the runway extension.

ROYAL AIR FORCE STATION · SELETAR
WE·WATCH·ALL·AROUND

ROYAL AIR FORCE STATION · SHARJAH
MIN AL-BARR ILA AL-SAMA

ROYAL AIR FORCE STATION · SOUTH CERNEY ·
STEADFAST

ROYAL AIR FORCE STATION · SPADEADAM ·
SI VIS PAREM PARA BELLUM

ROYAL AIR FORCE STATION · STEAMER POINT ·
PRO PLURIMUS ADASTO

ROYAL AIR FORCE STATION · SHAWBURY
DOCEO DUCO VOLO

ROYAL AIR FORCE STATION · STAXTON WOLD ·
VIGILAMUS ET DEFENDIMUS

ROYAL AIR FORCE STATION · STORNOWAY
LEAD AND GUIDE

ROYAL AIR FORCE STATION · STRADISHALL ·
VIRES DE CÆLO

ROYAL AIR FORCE STATION · SWANTON MORLEY ·
STEADFAST TO SERVE

SELETAR (1/30) **Badge** (3/40) On a pall couped and reversed gules three eastern crowns one and two Or. **Link** The badge is based upon that of the Straits Settlements and therefore indicative of the location with the *crowns* representing the Straights Settlements, Ceylon and Hong Kong all of which are in the orbit of the station.

SHARJAH (1/5/43) **Badge** (8/62) In front of a khunjar sable detailed Or an Arabian fort Or. **Motto** (A) From the land to the sky **Link** The *fort* represents a base for operations, s taging post and a support base all being roles undertaken by the station. The *khunjar* is a local weapon and indicative of the location and the readiness to fight.

SOUTH CERNEY (14/7/37) **Badge** (10/52) A Roman helmet Or plumed gules. **Link** The station is near Cirencester which has Roman connections.

SHAWBURY Badge (12/86) A roundel azure environed of an annulet Or surmounted of three lions faces 2 and 1 **Motto** (L) I teach, I guide , I fly. **Link** The *lions* come from the Arms of the Borough of Shrewsbury, close to the station, and represent not only the location but also the three major units CALTS, 2FTS and CFS(H) based there. The annulet symbolises the globe and the student who come from all over the world to the station.

SPADEADAM (12/76) **Badge** (4/84) The head of a roebuck proper set in front of an escallop argent. **Motto** (L) If you seek peace be ready for war. **Link** The *escallop* is symbolic of the radar reflectors used and also indicate the location of the unit being from the Arms of the Dacre family whose seat was at Gilsand. The *roebuck* is suggestive of the resident units who have to be observant and speedy in respect of their duties

STAXTON WOLD History In use since 12/39 but not a station until 1/4/74 **Badge** (4/78) In front of two arrows gules in saltire points upwards a roundel per pale argent and sable charged with a cresset counter charged and enflamed gules. **Motto** (L) We watch and we ward. **Link** The *cresset* is a warning device suitable for inclusion in the badge of a radar unit. It also perpetuates the link with RAF Patrington which was the previous parent station. The *arrows* represent active defence

STEAMER POINT (1/8/45) **Badge** (1954) A roundel barry wavy of eight the top four bars Or and azure the bottom four argent and azure the whole irradiated Or. **Motto** (L) I stand ready on behalf of many. **Link** The *water barry wavy* alludes to the location of the station on the Persian Gulf whilst the *irradiation* symbolises the desert, the heat and the sun.

STORNOWAY (6/41) **Badge** (2/45) In front of a beacon fired a dexter hand grasping another in fesse. **Link** The function of the unit is the guidance of aircraft from the United States and Canada to the south. The *clasped hands* equate to the friendship between the two areas whilst the *beacon* represents the guidance system used.

STRADISHALL (3/2/38) **Badge** (12/55) A birdbolt and an arrow both Or in saltire enfiled by a circlet argent **Motto** (L) Strength from the sky. **Link** The *birdbolt and arrow* represent the cannon and machine guns used by fighter aircraft which flew from the station whilst the *circlet* is indicative of the care provided by the station to the squadrons.

SWANTON MORLEY (17/9/40) **Badge** (10/80) In front of an annulet azure enfiling two ancient crowns in fess Or a stags head proper armed sable affronty gorged with a like crown. **Link** The badge is similar to that of the Arms of the town of East Dereham, close to the station.

ROYAL AIR FORCE STATION SYERSTON — PRAESTA IN OFFICIIS

ROYAL AIR FORCE STATION — SYLT — UNSWERVING

ROYAL AIR FORCE STATION TA KALI — EQUITES NOSTRI ARMA SUMUNT

ROYAL AIR FORCE STATION TANGMERE — ATTACK TO DEFEND

ROYAL AIR FORCE STATION TENGAH — CHERGAS

ROYAL AIR FORCE STATION THORNEY ISLAND — FLY TO ASSIST

ROYAL AIR FORCE STATION TOPCLIFFE — QUI OPERIT CAELUM

ROYAL AIR FORCE STATION TURNHOUSE — DORIENS DEFENDE

ROYAL AIR FORCE STATION UPAVON — IN PRINCIPIO ET SEMPER

ROYAL AIR FORCE STATION UPWOOD — PRO ARIS ET FOCIS

ROYAL AIR FORCE STATION UXBRIDGE — JUVENTUTEM FORMAMUS

SYERSTON (12/4/39) **Badge** (1/67) Surmounting a representation in grey of the ruins of Newark Castle two flashes of lightning in saltire Or at the points and in front thereof a torch argent enflamed gules/Or. **Motto** (L) Excel in duties **Link** The *castle* remembers the granting of the Freedom of the Newark to the station whilst the *flashes* allude to the wartime bomber station role. The present role of training is represented by the *torch*

SYLT History Opened 7/45 and closed 2/48 **Badge** (1/48) In front of a lighthouse argent a hand proper couped at the wrist holding a sword erect azure/Or. **Link** The *lighthouse* is from the Arms of Westerland, the largest town on Sylt. It also alludes to the Air Sea Rescue role that the station had for the area. The *hand and sword* signify the Armament Practice Camp role which was also undertaken.

TA KALI (11/40) **Badge** (1/43) In front of a maltese cross a roundel chequy thereon a demi-knight in armour affrontee. **Motto** (L) Our knights take up their arms **Link** All the components have links with the island of Malta

TANGMERE (23/11/26) **Badge** (7/53) In front of two swords in saltire argent/Or a lion passant guardant Or. **Link** The *swords* represent the day and night fighter role of the station whilst the *lion* comes from the Arms of the nearby City of Chichester.

TENGAH (5/3/38) **Badge** (2/51) An Argus pheasant proper. **Motto** (L) Alert **Link** The *pheasant* is a bird common to the sub-jungles of Malaya.

THORNEY ISLAND (3/2/38) **Badge** (9/71) On a base of thorn branches sable a lapwing proper. **Link** The *lapwing* frequents the airfield and its environs and is therefore indicative of the area. The *thorns* are a play upon the name of the station.

TOPCLIFFE (1/9/40) **Badge** (2/57) In front of a York rose a bugle horn proper. **Motto** (L) Who covereth the heavens **Link** The *horn* represents the Wakemans Horn of Ripon which was an alarm of danger symbolising the watchfulness of the unit whilst the *rose* is indicative of the location of the unit in Yorkshire.

TURNHOUSE (4/8/36) **Badge** (11/54) In front of a saltire an eagles head erased **Motto** (L) In striking, defend **Link** The *saltire* is indicative of the location of the unit in Scotland whilst the *eagle's head* alludes to the role of the station as a host to fighter squadrons.

UPAVON (15/15/12) **Badge** (4/61) A pterodactyl rising from rocks. **Motto** In the beginning and always **Link** Being one of the oldest RAF Stations in the country the unit has the *pterodactyl*, an early flying creature to symbolise the activities undertaken during the birth of miltary aviation. The *rocks* represent Stonehenge which is nearby.

UPWOOD (26/1/37) **Badge** (12/55) On a mount a hurst of oak trees the whole surmounted of a lion rampant. **Motto** (L) For health and home **Link** The *hurst* alludes to a nearby oak grove reputed to have hidden Charles I whilst this association is continued with the *lion* which comes from the Arms of the Cromwell family who were resident in the area.

UXBRIDGE History Formed 27/11/42 from No 1 RAF Depot. **Badge** (4/53) In front of a bugle a pace-stick. **Motto** (L) We form youth **Link** The *pace-stick* is the drill sergeants symbol and indicative of the basic training given to many hundreds of recruits who received their basic training on the station. The *bugle* is to remember the Central Band also stationed at the base.

ROYAL AIR FORCE STATION VALLEY — IN ADVERSIS PERFUGIUM

ROYAL AIR FORCE STATION WADDINGTON — FOR FAITH AND FREEDOM

ROYAL AIR FORCE STATION WARTLING — DETECTA DESTRUANTUR

ROYAL AIR FORCE STATION WATTISHAM — SUPRA MARE SUPRA TERRAMQUE

ROYAL AIR FORCE STATION WEST DRAYTON — PROTECT

ROYAL AIR FORCE STATION WATERBEACH — FLORES VIRTUTE CAPESSO

ROYAL AIR FORCE STATION WATTON — ADJUTORES MULTOREM

ROYAL AIR FORCE STATION WEST KIRBY — STRIVE TO EQUAL

ROYAL AIR FORCE STATION WEST MALLING — PORTAM CUSTODIMUS

ROYAL AIR FORCE STATION WEST RAYNHAM — PROBITATE ET LABORE

VALLEY History Formed 1/2/41 as Rhosneigr but renamed Valley on 5/4/41 **Badge** A dragon rampant holding a portcullis. **Motto** (L) Refuge in adversity. **Link** The *dragon* represents the location of the station in Wales whilst the *portcullis* is indicative of the ever-open role of the station as a Master Diversion Airfield.

WADDINGTON (12/3/37) **Badge** (1953) Issuant from clouds argent a representation of the tower of Lincoln Cathedral Or. **Link** The *tower* is a welcome sight for pilots, often being visible above the morning and evening mists which cover all but the tallest landmarks.

WARTLING (30/10/41) **Badge** In front of a chained portcullis Or a wild cat's face sable. **Motto** (L) Let that which has been found be destroyed **Link** The *portcullis* is indicative of defence whilst the *wild cat* reminds us that the station is on constant alert.

WATERBEACH (1/1/40) **Badge** A rose gules and a gilliflower purpure in saltire **Motto** In courage I aim at the highest **Link** The flowers were the rent paid for Waterbeach Manor and Abbey

WATTISHAM (4/39) **Badge** (8/40) An eagle sable armed gules perched on a demi-ship Or. **Motto** (L) Above the sea and above the land. **Link** The *demi-ship* comes from the Arms of Ipswich to which the station is affiliated whilst the *eagle* alludes to RAF operations.

WATTON (10/6/63) **Badge** (11/65) In front of a roundel azure with a bend ermine an iron age sword argent hilted Or **Motto** (L) In support of many **Link** The *hurt* alludes to the blue skies over Norfolk, the *bend* comes from the Arms of the County whilst the *sword* has associations with the Iceni tribe who were resident in the area.

WEST DRAYTON (1/9/24) **Badge** (11/72) In front of two shepherds crooks Or turned inwards and in saltire a word argent hilted Or erect between two flashes of lightning gules fesswise **Link** The *crooks* are are link with the air traffic control role of the station whilst the *sword* alludes to the air defence role. The *flashes* indicate the part which electronics plays in modern communications.

WEST KIRBY A badge for this unit of 'In front of a wreath of laurel a sword in pale argent/Or the hilt held by two right hands proper' was approved by Queen Elizabeth in 4/52 but approval was withdrawn by the Air Ministry when it was found that there was no actual Station of the name but only No 5 School of Recruit Training in residence. The use of the Reserve Command badge with the name RAF West Kirby in the frame was approved. The reasons for the badge components were; the *sword* the RAF, the *laurels* the best training given and the *two right hands* the passing on of their knowledge from instructors to recruits.

WEST MALLING (6/40) **Badge** (7/52) In front of a portcullis a representation of St Leonards Tower, West Malling. **Motto** (L) We guard the gate. **Link** The *tower* represents the defence given to the area by the station whilst the *portcullis* coming from the badge of Fighter Command indicates that the aircraft from West Malling form part of a defensive barrier. It also is a link to the Command.

WEST RAYNHAM History Formed in 1939 the station only became such officially on 12/10/62 **Badge** (7/64) In front of a Suffolk Punches head (brown) erased at the neck charged with a grenade sable fired gules/Or a sword argent hilted Or in bend sinister. **Motto** (L) By honesty and toil **Link** The *grenade and sword* represent the bomber and fighter aircraft based at the station whilst the *head* is that of a strong animal native to the area.

ROYAL AIR FORCE STATION
WILDENRATH
IMMER BEREIT

ROYAL AIR FORCE STATION
WITTERING
STRENGTH IS FREEDOM

ROYAL AIR FORCE STATION
WYTHALL
SEEK HEAR AND GUIDE

ROYAL AIR FORCE STATION
WYTON
VERUM EXQUIRO

AEROBATIC TEAM
ROYAL AIR FORCE
ECLAT

WILDENRATH Badge In front of an annulet vert surmounted by four fir cones vert points outwards a harrier in hovering flight. **Motto** (G) Always ready **Link** The *annulet* represent the base whilst the *fir cones* indicate its location in a wooded area. The cones are at the four cardinal points to signify the watchfulness of the station on all sides. The *harrier* alludes to the Hawker Harrier aircraft operated from the station.

WITTERING (11/4/38) **Badge** (8/55) A lion rampant triple queued collared with a chain detached therefrom **Link** The *lion* comes from the Arms of the town of Stamford which is close by. The *detached collar* indicates that units are released from the station to operate independently away from base whilst the *three tails* on the lion allude to the three wings and three commands which have been part of the station's history.

WYTHALL (2/41) **Badge** (8/55) A torch azure enfiled by a chain Or. **Link** The *torch* represents the training role of the station with the *flame* reminding that radio navigation aids are the main concern. It also is indicative of the Signals Unit at the base. The 13 links in the *chain* are representative of the 13 Signals Units for which the station is responsible.

WYTON (30/7/36) **Badge** (10/56) A sun in splendour Or surmounted of a bow sable fesswise the strings uppermost overall a sword argent hilted Or point upwards. **Motto** (L) Seek the truth. **Link** The *bow* is a play upon the name of the town of Huntingdon, which is close by. The *sun* is indicative of the light needed to undertake the photo-recconaissance role of the station whilst the *sword* reminds the personnel of their role in times of war.

AEROBATIC TEAM (Fairford 1/3/56) **Badge** (4/80) In front of a plate nine arrowheads gules each bendwise three, three and three. **Link** The red arrows are indicative of the name of the team whilst the shape of the design is representative of one of their display formations.

UKADGE SYSTEMS SUPPORT TEAM Note The initials stand for United Kingdom Air Defence Ground Environment. **Badge** (4/83) In front of an annulet wavy two flashes of lightning in saltire overall a sword erect the blade enfiled of an Astral crown. **Link** The *annulet* comes from the badge of Strike Command, the *flashes of lightning* allude to the role of electronics in computer systems, the *sword* is indicative of defence whilst the *Astral crown* is the RAF.

INDEX

INDEX   56

57

INDEX

INDEX

INDEX